SAXON
MATH

Course 3

Power Up
Workbook

Stephen Hake

Image Credits: (Paper background pieces) ©Kittichai/Shutterstock; (elephant) johan63/iStock/ Getty Images.

Printed in the U.S.A.

ISBN   978-1-328-49749-9

1 2 3 4 5 6 7 8 9 10   0982   26 25 24 23 22 21 20 19 18

4500708697   A B C D E F G

Dear Student,

We enjoy watching the adventures of "Super Heroes" because they have powers that they use for good. Power is the ability to get things done. We acquire power through concentrated effort and practice. We build powerful bodies with vigorous exercise and healthy living. We develop powerful minds by learning and using skills that help us understand the world around us and solve problems that come our way.

We can build our mathematical power in several ways. We can use our memory to store and instantly recall frequently used information. We can improve our ability to solve many kinds of problems mentally without using pencil and paper or a calculator. We can also expand the range of strategies we use to approach and solve new problems.

The Power Up section of each lesson in *Saxon Math Course 3* is designed to build your mathematical power. Each Power Up has three parts: Facts Practice, Mental Math, and Problem Solving. The three parts are printed on every Power Up page where you will record your answers. This workbook contains a Power Up page for every lesson.

Facts Practice is like a race—write the answers as fast as you can without making mistakes. If the information in the Facts Practice is new to you, take time to study the information so that you can recall the facts quickly and can complete the exercise faster next time.

Mental Math is the ability to work with numbers in your head. This skill greatly improves with practice. Each lesson includes several mental math problems. Your teacher will read these to you or ask you to read them in your book. Do your best to find the answer to each problem without using pencil and paper, except to record your answers. Strong mental math ability will help you throughout your life.

Problem Solving is like a puzzle. You need to figure out how to solve each puzzle. There are many different strategies you can use to solve problems. There are also some questions you can ask yourself to better understand a problem and come up with a plan to solve it. Your teacher will guide you through the problem each day. Becoming a good problem solver is a superior skill that is highly rewarded.

The Power Ups will help you excel at math and acquire math power that will serve you well for the rest of your life.

Stephen Hake
Temple City, California

Power Up Workbook

Name _____

Power Up Facts	# Possible	Time and Score
A 40 Multiplication Facts	40	
B 40 Multiplication Facts	40	
C Reducing Fractions	20	
D Exponents	20	
E Square Roots	20	
F Improper Fractions and Mixed Numbers	20	
G Laws of Exponents	12	
H Converting Fractions to Decimals	20	
I Operations with Integers	12	
J Circles	10	
K One-Step Equations	20	
L Scientific Notation	12	
M Converting Percents to Fractions	20	
N Proportions	12	
O Angle Relationships	6	
P Multiplying and Dividing in Scientific Notation	10	
Q Add, Subtract, Multiply, and Divide Terms	20	
R Converting from Percents to Decimals and Fractions	24	
S U.S. Customary Measurement Facts	18	
T Converting from Fractions to Decimals and Percents	24	
U Formulas	9	
V Metric Measurement Facts	18	
W Simplify Square Roots	12	
X Multiplying Binomials	12	

(Time and Score header note: time / # correct)

Saxon Math Course 3

Facts   Multiply.

9 × 9	7 × 3	9 × 2	7 × 4	0 × 8	5 × 2	12 × 12	9 × 8	3 × 3	6 × 5
11 × 11	4 × 2	7 × 6	8 × 8	9 × 3	9 × 7	5 × 4	8 × 6	3 × 2	9 × 4
7 × 2	5 × 5	4 × 3	9 × 5	2 × 2	7 × 5	8 × 4	6 × 3	8 × 7	6 × 4
4 × 4	9 × 6	8 × 2	8 × 3	10 × 10	6 × 6	5 × 3	7 × 7	6 × 2	8 × 5

Mental Math

a.	**b.**	**c.**	**d.**
e.	**f.**	**g.**	**h.**

Problem Solving

Understand

What information am I given?

What am I asked to find or do?

- -

Plan

How can I use the information I am given?

Which strategy should I try?

- -

Solve

Did I follow the plan?

Did I show my work?

Did I write the answer?

- -

Check

Did I use the correct information?

Did I do what was asked?

Is my answer reasonable?

Facts   Multiply.

9 × 9	7 × 3	9 × 2	7 × 4	0 × 8	5 × 2	12 × 12	9 × 8	3 × 3	6 × 5
11 × 11	4 × 2	7 × 6	8 × 8	9 × 3	9 × 7	5 × 4	8 × 6	3 × 2	9 × 4
7 × 2	5 × 5	4 × 3	9 × 5	2 × 2	7 × 5	8 × 4	6 × 3	8 × 7	6 × 4
4 × 4	9 × 6	8 × 2	8 × 3	10 × 10	6 × 6	5 × 3	7 × 7	6 × 2	8 × 5

Mental Math

a.	b.	c.	d.
e.	f.	g.	h.

Problem Solving

Understand
What information am I given?
What am I asked to find or do?

Plan
How can I use the information I am given?
Which strategy should I try?

Solve
Did I follow the plan?
Did I show my work?
Did I write the answer?

Check
Did I use the correct information?
Did I do what was asked?
Is my answer reasonable?

Facts   Multiply.

9 × 9	7 × 3	9 × 2	7 × 4	0 × 8	5 × 2	12 × 12	9 × 8	3 × 3	6 × 5
11 × 11	4 × 2	7 × 6	8 × 8	9 × 3	9 × 7	5 × 4	8 × 6	3 × 2	9 × 4
7 × 2	5 × 5	4 × 3	9 × 5	2 × 2	7 × 5	8 × 4	6 × 3	8 × 7	6 × 4
4 × 4	9 × 6	8 × 2	8 × 3	10 × 10	6 × 6	5 × 3	7 × 7	6 × 2	8 × 5

Mental Math

a.	**b.**	**c.**	**d.**
e.	**f.**	**g.**	**h.**

Problem Solving

Understand

What information am I given?
What am I asked to find or do?

- -

Plan

How can I use the information I am given?
Which strategy should I try?

- -

Solve

Did I follow the plan?
Did I show my work?
Did I write the answer?

- -

Check

Did I use the correct information?
Did I do what was asked?
Is my answer reasonable?

Facts   Multiply.

9 ×9	7 ×3	9 ×2	7 ×4	0 ×8	5 ×2	12 ×12	9 ×8	3 ×3	6 ×5
11 ×11	4 ×2	7 ×6	8 ×8	9 ×3	9 ×7	5 ×4	8 ×6	3 ×2	9 ×4
7 ×2	5 ×5	4 ×3	9 ×5	2 ×2	7 ×5	8 ×4	6 ×3	8 ×7	6 ×4
4 ×4	9 ×6	8 ×2	8 ×3	10 ×10	6 ×6	5 ×3	7 ×7	6 ×2	8 ×5

Mental Math

a.	b.	c.	d.
e.	f.	g.	h.

Problem Solving

Understand
What information am I given?
What am I asked to find or do?

- -

Plan
How can I use the information I am given?
Which strategy should I try?

- -

Solve
Did I follow the plan?
Did I show my work?
Did I write the answer?

- -

Check
Did I use the correct information?
Did I do what was asked?
Is my answer reasonable?

Facts Multiply.

9 × 9	7 × 3	9 × 2	7 × 4	0 × 8	5 × 2	12 × 12	9 × 8	3 × 3	6 × 5
11 × 11	4 × 2	7 × 6	8 × 8	9 × 3	9 × 7	5 × 4	8 × 6	3 × 2	9 × 4
7 × 2	5 × 5	4 × 3	9 × 5	2 × 2	7 × 5	8 × 4	6 × 3	8 × 7	6 × 4
4 × 4	9 × 6	8 × 2	8 × 3	10 × 10	6 × 6	5 × 3	7 × 7	6 × 2	8 × 5

Mental Math

a.	b.	c.	d.
e.	f.	g.	h.

Problem Solving

Understand

What information am I given?
What am I asked to find or do?

- -

Plan

How can I use the information I am given?
Which strategy should I try?

- -

Solve

Did I follow the plan?
Did I show my work?
Did I write the answer?

- -

Check

Did I use the correct information?
Did I do what was asked?
Is my answer reasonable?

Facts   Multiply.

10 × 10	6 × 9	2 × 4	5 × 0	4 × 6	3 × 3	5 × 8	4 × 9	2 × 7	3 × 8
2 × 9	5 × 5	7 × 9	3 × 7	6 × 6	8 × 9	2 × 3	5 × 9	4 × 8	8 × 8
4 × 7	2 × 6	3 × 9	7 × 7	2 × 8	11 × 11	5 × 6	4 × 4	6 × 7	3 × 5
3 × 4	7 × 8	4 × 5	2 × 2	6 × 8	5 × 7	3 × 6	12 × 12	2 × 5	9 × 9

Mental Math

a.	**b.**	**c.**	**d.**
e.	**f.**	**g.**	**h.**

Problem Solving

Understand

What information am I given?

What am I asked to find or do?

Plan

How can I use the information I am given?

Which strategy should I try?

Solve

Did I follow the plan?

Did I show my work?

Did I write the answer?

Check

Did I use the correct information?

Did I do what was asked?

Is my answer reasonable?

Name _____ Time _____

Facts   Multiply.

10 × 10	6 × 9	2 × 4	5 × 0	4 × 6	3 × 3	5 × 8	4 × 9	2 × 7	3 × 8
2 × 9	5 × 5	7 × 9	3 × 7	6 × 6	8 × 9	2 × 3	5 × 9	4 × 8	8 × 8
4 × 7	2 × 6	3 × 9	7 × 7	2 × 8	11 × 11	5 × 6	4 × 4	6 × 7	3 × 5
3 × 4	7 × 8	4 × 5	2 × 2	6 × 8	5 × 7	3 × 6	12 × 12	2 × 5	9 × 9

Mental Math

a.	**b.**	**c.**	**d.**
e.	**f.**	**g.**	**h.**

Problem Solving

Understand

What information am I given?
What am I asked to find or do?

Plan

How can I use the information I am given?
Which strategy should I try?

Solve

Did I follow the plan?
Did I show my work?
Did I write the answer?

Check

Did I use the correct information?
Did I do what was asked?
Is my answer reasonable?

Name _____ Time _____

Facts   Multiply.

10 × 10	6 × 9	2 × 4	5 × 0	4 × 6	3 × 3	5 × 8	4 × 9	2 × 7	3 × 8
2 × 9	5 × 5	7 × 9	3 × 7	6 × 6	8 × 9	2 × 3	5 × 9	4 × 8	8 × 8
4 × 7	2 × 6	3 × 9	7 × 7	2 × 8	11 × 11	5 × 6	4 × 4	6 × 7	3 × 5
3 × 4	7 × 8	4 × 5	2 × 2	6 × 8	5 × 7	3 × 6	12 × 12	2 × 5	9 × 9

Mental Math

a.	b.	c.	d.
e.	f.	g.	h.

Problem Solving

Understand

What information am I given?
What am I asked to find or do?

Plan

How can I use the information I am given?
Which strategy should I try?

Solve

Did I follow the plan?
Did I show my work?
Did I write the answer?

Check

Did I use the correct information?
Did I do what was asked?
Is my answer reasonable?

© Houghton Mifflin Harcourt Publishing Company and Stephen Hake

Saxon Math Course 3

Facts   Multiply.

10 × 10	6 × 9	2 × 4	5 × 0	4 × 6	3 × 3	5 × 8	4 × 9	2 × 7	3 × 8
2 × 9	5 × 5	7 × 9	3 × 7	6 × 6	8 × 9	2 × 3	5 × 9	4 × 8	8 × 8
4 × 7	2 × 6	3 × 9	7 × 7	2 × 8	11 × 11	5 × 6	4 × 4	6 × 7	3 × 5
3 × 4	7 × 8	4 × 5	2 × 2	6 × 8	5 × 7	3 × 6	12 × 12	2 × 5	9 × 9

Mental Math

a.	b.	c.	d.
e.	f.	g.	h.

Problem Solving

Understand
What information am I given?
What am I asked to find or do?

Plan
How can I use the information I am given?
Which strategy should I try?

Solve
Did I follow the plan?
Did I show my work?
Did I write the answer?

Check
Did I use the correct information?
Did I do what was asked?
Is my answer reasonable?

Facts   Multiply.

10 × 10	6 × 9	2 × 4	5 × 0	4 × 6	3 × 3	5 × 8	4 × 9	2 × 7	3 × 8
2 × 9	5 × 5	7 × 9	3 × 7	6 × 6	8 × 9	2 × 3	5 × 9	4 × 8	8 × 8
4 × 7	2 × 6	3 × 9	7 × 7	2 × 8	11 × 11	5 × 6	4 × 4	6 × 7	3 × 5
3 × 4	7 × 8	4 × 5	2 × 2	6 × 8	5 × 7	3 × 6	12 × 12	2 × 5	9 × 9

Mental Math

a.	**b.**	**c.**	**d.**
e.	**f.**	**g.**	**h.**

Problem Solving

Understand

What information am I given?
What am I asked to find or do?

- -

Plan

How can I use the information I am given?
Which strategy should I try?

- -

Solve

Did I follow the plan?
Did I show my work?
Did I write the answer?

- -

Check

Did I use the correct information?
Did I do what was asked?
Is my answer reasonable?

Name _____ Time _____

Facts   Reduce each fraction to lowest terms.

$\frac{2}{10} =$	$\frac{2}{8} =$	$\frac{3}{9} =$	$\frac{8}{10} =$	$\frac{3}{6} =$
$\frac{6}{8} =$	$\frac{3}{12} =$	$\frac{2}{4} =$	$\frac{6}{12} =$	$\frac{9}{12} =$
$\frac{4}{12} =$	$\frac{2}{6} =$	$\frac{8}{16} =$	$\frac{5}{10} =$	$\frac{6}{9} =$
$\frac{4}{8} =$	$\frac{8}{12} =$	$\frac{4}{10} =$	$\frac{4}{6} =$	$\frac{6}{10} =$

Mental Math

a.	b.	c.	d.
e.	f.	g.	h.

Problem Solving

Understand
What information am I given?
What am I asked to find or do?

Plan
How can I use the information I am given?
Which strategy should I try?

Solve
Did I follow the plan?
Did I show my work?
Did I write the answer?

Check
Did I use the correct information?
Did I do what was asked?
Is my answer reasonable?

© Houghton Mifflin Harcourt Publishing Company and Stephen Hake

Name _____ Time _____

Facts Reduce each fraction to lowest terms.

$\frac{2}{10} =$	$\frac{2}{8} =$	$\frac{3}{9} =$	$\frac{8}{10} =$	$\frac{3}{6} =$
$\frac{6}{8} =$	$\frac{3}{12} =$	$\frac{2}{4} =$	$\frac{6}{12} =$	$\frac{9}{12} =$
$\frac{4}{12} =$	$\frac{2}{6} =$	$\frac{8}{16} =$	$\frac{5}{10} =$	$\frac{6}{9} =$
$\frac{4}{8} =$	$\frac{8}{12} =$	$\frac{4}{10} =$	$\frac{4}{6} =$	$\frac{6}{10} =$

Mental Math

a.	**b.**	**c.**	**d.**
e.	**f.**	**g.**	**h.**

Problem Solving

Understand
What information am I given?
What am I asked to find or do?

Plan
How can I use the information I am given?
Which strategy should I try?

Solve
Did I follow the plan?
Did I show my work?
Did I write the answer?

Check
Did I use the correct information?
Did I do what was asked?
Is my answer reasonable?

© Houghton Mifflin Harcourt Publishing Company and Stephen Hake

Facts   Reduce each fraction to lowest terms.

$\frac{2}{10} =$	$\frac{2}{8} =$	$\frac{3}{9} =$	$\frac{8}{10} =$	$\frac{3}{6} =$
$\frac{6}{8} =$	$\frac{3}{12} =$	$\frac{2}{4} =$	$\frac{6}{12} =$	$\frac{9}{12} =$
$\frac{4}{12} =$	$\frac{2}{6} =$	$\frac{8}{16} =$	$\frac{5}{10} =$	$\frac{6}{9} =$
$\frac{4}{8} =$	$\frac{8}{12} =$	$\frac{4}{10} =$	$\frac{4}{6} =$	$\frac{6}{10} =$

Mental Math

a.	**b.**	**c.**	**d.**
e.	**f.**	**g.**	**h.**

Problem Solving

Understand
What information am I given?
What am I asked to find or do?

- -

Plan
How can I use the information I am given?
Which strategy should I try?

- -

Solve
Did I follow the plan?
Did I show my work?
Did I write the answer?

- -

Check
Did I use the correct information?
Did I do what was asked?
Is my answer reasonable?

Facts	Reduce each fraction to lowest terms.

$\frac{2}{10} =$	$\frac{2}{8} =$	$\frac{3}{9} =$	$\frac{8}{10} =$	$\frac{3}{6} =$
$\frac{6}{8} =$	$\frac{3}{12} =$	$\frac{2}{4} =$	$\frac{6}{12} =$	$\frac{9}{12} =$
$\frac{4}{12} =$	$\frac{2}{6} =$	$\frac{8}{16} =$	$\frac{5}{10} =$	$\frac{6}{9} =$
$\frac{4}{8} =$	$\frac{8}{12} =$	$\frac{4}{10} =$	$\frac{4}{6} =$	$\frac{6}{10} =$

Mental Math			
a.	b.	c.	d.
e.	f.	g.	h.

Problem Solving

Understand
What information am I given?
What am I asked to find or do?

- -

Plan
How can I use the information I am given?
Which strategy should I try?

- -

Solve
Did I follow the plan?
Did I show my work?
Did I write the answer?

- -

Check
Did I use the correct information?
Did I do what was asked?
Is my answer reasonable?

| Facts | Reduce each fraction to lowest terms. |

$\frac{2}{10} =$	$\frac{2}{8} =$	$\frac{3}{9} =$	$\frac{8}{10} =$	$\frac{3}{6} =$
$\frac{6}{8} =$	$\frac{3}{12} =$	$\frac{2}{4} =$	$\frac{6}{12} =$	$\frac{9}{12} =$
$\frac{4}{12} =$	$\frac{2}{6} =$	$\frac{8}{16} =$	$\frac{5}{10} =$	$\frac{6}{9} =$
$\frac{4}{8} =$	$\frac{8}{12} =$	$\frac{4}{10} =$	$\frac{4}{6} =$	$\frac{6}{10} =$

Mental Math

a.	b.	c.	d.
e.	f.	g.	h.

Problem Solving

Understand
What information am I given?
What am I asked to find or do?

- -

Plan
How can I use the information I am given?
Which strategy should I try?

- -

Solve
Did I follow the plan?
Did I show my work?
Did I write the answer?

- -

Check
Did I use the correct information?
Did I do what was asked?
Is my answer reasonable?

Facts	Simplify each power.

$10^2 =$	$20^2 =$	$2^2 =$	$2^3 =$	$5^2 =$
$3^2 =$	$6^2 =$	$9^2 =$	$4^2 =$	$8^2 =$
$7^2 =$	$1^2 =$	$11^2 =$	$30^2 =$	$10^3 =$
$12^2 =$	$13^2 =$	$25^2 =$	$15^2 =$	$\left(\dfrac{1}{2}\right)^2 =$

Mental Math			
a.	**b.**	**c.**	**d.**
e.	**f.**	**g.**	**h.**

Problem Solving

Understand

What information am I given?

What am I asked to find or do?

Plan

How can I use the information I am given?

Which strategy should I try?

Solve

Did I follow the plan?

Did I show my work?

Did I write the answer?

Check

Did I use the correct information?

Did I do what was asked?

Is my answer reasonable?

© Houghton Mifflin Harcourt Publishing Company and Stephen Hake

Facts	Simplify each power.			
$10^2 =$	$20^2 =$	$2^2 =$	$2^3 =$	$5^2 =$
$3^2 =$	$6^2 =$	$9^2 =$	$4^2 =$	$8^2 =$
$7^2 =$	$1^2 =$	$11^2 =$	$30^2 =$	$10^3 =$
$12^2 =$	$13^2 =$	$25^2 =$	$15^2 =$	$\left(\frac{1}{2}\right)^2 =$

Mental Math

a.	b.	c.	d.
e.	f.	g.	h.

Problem Solving

Understand

What information am I given?

What am I asked to find or do?

- -

Plan

How can I use the information I am given?

Which strategy should I try?

- -

Solve

Did I follow the plan?

Did I show my work?

Did I write the answer?

- -

Check

Did I use the correct information?

Did I do what was asked?

Is my answer reasonable?

Facts   Simplify each power.

$10^2 =$	$20^2 =$	$2^2 =$	$2^3 =$	$5^2 =$
$3^2 =$	$6^2 =$	$9^2 =$	$4^2 =$	$8^2 =$
$7^2 =$	$1^2 =$	$11^2 =$	$30^2 =$	$10^3 =$
$12^2 =$	$13^2 =$	$25^2 =$	$15^2 =$	$\left(\frac{1}{2}\right)^2 =$

Mental Math

a.	**b.**	**c.**	**d.**
e.	**f.**	**g.**	**h.**

Problem Solving

Understand

What information am I given?

What am I asked to find or do?

- -

Plan

How can I use the information I am given?

Which strategy should I try?

- -

Solve

Did I follow the plan?

Did I show my work?

Did I write the answer?

- -

Check

Did I use the correct information?

Did I do what was asked?

Is my answer reasonable?

Facts   Simplify each power.

$10^2 =$	$20^2 =$	$2^2 =$	$2^3 =$	$5^2 =$
$3^2 =$	$6^2 =$	$9^2 =$	$4^2 =$	$8^2 =$
$7^2 =$	$1^2 =$	$11^2 =$	$30^2 =$	$10^3 =$
$12^2 =$	$13^2 =$	$25^2 =$	$15^2 =$	$\left(\dfrac{1}{2}\right)^2 =$

Mental Math

a.	**b.**	**c.**	**d.**
e.	**f.**	**g.**	**h.**

Problem Solving

Understand
What information am I given?
What am I asked to find or do?

- -

Plan
How can I use the information I am given?
Which strategy should I try?

- -

Solve
Did I follow the plan?
Did I show my work?
Did I write the answer?

- -

Check
Did I use the correct information?
Did I do what was asked?
Is my answer reasonable?

Facts Simplify each power.

$10^2 =$	$20^2 =$	$2^2 =$	$2^3 =$	$5^2 =$
$3^2 =$	$6^2 =$	$9^2 =$	$4^2 =$	$8^2 =$
$7^2 =$	$1^2 =$	$11^2 =$	$30^2 =$	$10^3 =$
$12^2 =$	$13^2 =$	$25^2 =$	$15^2 =$	$\left(\frac{1}{2}\right)^2 =$

Mental Math

a.	**b.**	**c.**	**d.**
e.	**f.**	**g.**	**h.**

Problem Solving

Understand

What information am I given?
What am I asked to find or do?

- -

Plan

How can I use the information I am given?
Which strategy should I try?

- -

Solve

Did I follow the plan?
Did I show my work?
Did I write the answer?

- -

Check

Did I use the correct information?
Did I do what was asked?
Is my answer reasonable?

Saxon Math Course 3

Facts   Simplify each root.

$\sqrt{81}$ =	$\sqrt{25}$ =	$\sqrt{1}$ =	$\sqrt{4}$ =	$\sqrt{49}$ =
$\sqrt{16}$ =	$\sqrt{64}$ =	$\sqrt{100}$ =	$\sqrt{144}$ =	$\sqrt{9}$ =
$\sqrt{36}$ =	$\sqrt{121}$ =	$\sqrt{400}$ =	$\sqrt{625}$ =	$\sqrt{225}$ =
$\sqrt{900}$ =	$\sqrt{\frac{1}{4}}$ =	$\sqrt{\frac{1}{9}}$ =	$\sqrt{2}$ ≈	$\sqrt{3}$ ≈

Mental Math

a.	**b.**	**c.**	**d.**
e.	**f.**	**g.**	**h.**

Problem Solving

Understand

What information am I given?

What am I asked to find or do?

- -

Plan

How can I use the information I am given?

Which strategy should I try?

- -

Solve

Did I follow the plan?

Did I show my work?

Did I write the answer?

- -

Check

Did I use the correct information?

Did I do what was asked?

Is my answer reasonable?

Facts	Simplify each root.

$\sqrt{81}$ =	$\sqrt{25}$ =	$\sqrt{1}$ =	$\sqrt{4}$ =	$\sqrt{49}$ =
$\sqrt{16}$ =	$\sqrt{64}$ =	$\sqrt{100}$ =	$\sqrt{144}$ =	$\sqrt{9}$ =
$\sqrt{36}$ =	$\sqrt{121}$ =	$\sqrt{400}$ =	$\sqrt{625}$ =	$\sqrt{225}$ =
$\sqrt{900}$ =	$\sqrt{\dfrac{1}{4}}$ =	$\sqrt{\dfrac{1}{9}}$ =	$\sqrt{2}$ ≈	$\sqrt{3}$ ≈

Mental Math

a.	**b.**	**c.**	**d.**
e.	**f.**	**g.**	**h.**

Problem Solving

Understand

What information am I given?
What am I asked to find or do?

- -

Plan

How can I use the information I am given?
Which strategy should I try?

- -

Solve

Did I follow the plan?
Did I show my work?
Did I write the answer?

- -

Check

Did I use the correct information?
Did I do what was asked?
Is my answer reasonable?

© Houghton Mifflin Harcourt Publishing Company and Stephen Hake

Facts	Simplify each root.			
$\sqrt{81}$ =	$\sqrt{25}$ =	$\sqrt{1}$ =	$\sqrt{4}$ =	$\sqrt{49}$ =
$\sqrt{16}$ =	$\sqrt{64}$ =	$\sqrt{100}$ =	$\sqrt{144}$ =	$\sqrt{9}$ =
$\sqrt{36}$ =	$\sqrt{121}$ =	$\sqrt{400}$ =	$\sqrt{625}$ =	$\sqrt{225}$ =
$\sqrt{900}$ =	$\sqrt{\dfrac{1}{4}}$ =	$\sqrt{\dfrac{1}{9}}$ =	$\sqrt{2}$ ≈	$\sqrt{3}$ ≈

Mental Math

a.	b.	c.	d.
e.	f.	g.	h.

Problem Solving

Understand

What information am I given?

What am I asked to find or do?

- -

Plan

How can I use the information I am given?

Which strategy should I try?

- -

Solve

Did I follow the plan?

Did I show my work?

Did I write the answer?

- -

Check

Did I use the correct information?

Did I do what was asked?

Is my answer reasonable?

Facts — Simplify each root.

$\sqrt{81} =$	$\sqrt{25} =$	$\sqrt{1} =$	$\sqrt{4} =$	$\sqrt{49} =$
$\sqrt{16} =$	$\sqrt{64} =$	$\sqrt{100} =$	$\sqrt{144} =$	$\sqrt{9} =$
$\sqrt{36} =$	$\sqrt{121} =$	$\sqrt{400} =$	$\sqrt{625} =$	$\sqrt{225} =$
$\sqrt{900} =$	$\sqrt{\dfrac{1}{4}} =$	$\sqrt{\dfrac{1}{9}} =$	$\sqrt{2} \approx$	$\sqrt{3} \approx$

Mental Math

a.	**b.**	**c.**	**d.**
e.	**f.**	**g.**	**h.**

Problem Solving

Understand

What information am I given?

What am I asked to find or do?

- -

Plan

How can I use the information I am given?

Which strategy should I try?

- -

Solve

Did I follow the plan?

Did I show my work?

Did I write the answer?

- -

Check

Did I use the correct information?

Did I do what was asked?

Is my answer reasonable?

| Facts | Simplify each root. |

$\sqrt{81} =$	$\sqrt{25} =$	$\sqrt{1} =$	$\sqrt{4} =$	$\sqrt{49} =$
$\sqrt{16} =$	$\sqrt{64} =$	$\sqrt{100} =$	$\sqrt{144} =$	$\sqrt{9} =$
$\sqrt{36} =$	$\sqrt{121} =$	$\sqrt{400} =$	$\sqrt{625} =$	$\sqrt{225} =$
$\sqrt{900} =$	$\sqrt{\dfrac{1}{4}} =$	$\sqrt{\dfrac{1}{9}} =$	$\sqrt{2} \approx$	$\sqrt{3} \approx$

Mental Math

a.	b.	c.	d.
e.	f.	g.	h.

Problem Solving

Understand

What information am I given?

What am I asked to find or do?

- -

Plan

How can I use the information I am given?

Which strategy should I try?

- -

Solve

Did I follow the plan?

Did I show my work?

Did I write the answer?

- -

Check

Did I use the correct information?

Did I do what was asked?

Is my answer reasonable?

Facts   Express each mixed number as an improper fraction.

$3\frac{1}{3} =$	$1\frac{3}{4} =$	$7\frac{1}{2} =$	$2\frac{2}{3} =$	$2\frac{4}{5} =$
$10\frac{1}{2} =$	$1\frac{7}{8} =$	$33\frac{1}{3} =$	$12\frac{1}{2} =$	$6\frac{2}{3} =$

Express each improper fraction as a mixed number or whole number.

$\frac{8}{4} =$	$\frac{11}{5} =$	$\frac{7}{2} =$	$\frac{14}{3} =$	$\frac{11}{4} =$
$\frac{16}{5} =$	$\frac{24}{6} =$	$\frac{23}{10} =$	$\frac{19}{6} =$	$\frac{16}{7} =$

Mental Math

a.	b.	c.	d.
e.	f.	g.	h.

Problem Solving

Understand

What information am I given?

What am I asked to find or do?

Plan

How can I use the information I am given?

Which strategy should I try?

Solve

Did I follow the plan?

Did I show my work?

Did I write the answer?

Check

Did I use the correct information?

Did I do what was asked?

Is my answer reasonable?

Facts   Express each mixed number as an improper fraction.

$3\frac{1}{3} =$	$1\frac{3}{4} =$	$7\frac{1}{2} =$	$2\frac{2}{3} =$	$2\frac{4}{5} =$
$10\frac{1}{2} =$	$1\frac{7}{8} =$	$33\frac{1}{3} =$	$12\frac{1}{2} =$	$6\frac{2}{3} =$

Express each improper fraction as a mixed number or whole number.

$\frac{8}{4} =$	$\frac{11}{5} =$	$\frac{7}{2} =$	$\frac{14}{3} =$	$\frac{11}{4} =$
$\frac{16}{5} =$	$\frac{24}{6} =$	$\frac{23}{10} =$	$\frac{19}{6} =$	$\frac{16}{7} =$

Mental Math

a.	b.	c.	d.
e.	f.	g.	h.

Problem Solving

Understand

What information am I given?

What am I asked to find or do?

Plan

How can I use the information I am given?

Which strategy should I try?

Solve

Did I follow the plan?

Did I show my work?

Did I write the answer?

Check

Did I use the correct information?

Did I do what was asked?

Is my answer reasonable?

Facts	Express each mixed number as an improper fraction.

$3\frac{1}{3} =$	$1\frac{3}{4} =$	$7\frac{1}{2} =$	$2\frac{2}{3} =$	$2\frac{4}{5} =$
$10\frac{1}{2} =$	$1\frac{7}{8} =$	$33\frac{1}{3} =$	$12\frac{1}{2} =$	$6\frac{2}{3} =$

Express each improper fraction as a mixed number or whole number.

$\frac{8}{4} =$	$\frac{11}{5} =$	$\frac{7}{2} =$	$\frac{14}{3} =$	$\frac{11}{4} =$
$\frac{16}{5} =$	$\frac{24}{6} =$	$\frac{23}{10} =$	$\frac{19}{6} =$	$\frac{16}{7} =$

Mental Math			
a.	**b.**	**c.**	**d.**
e.	**f.**	**g.**	**h.**

Problem Solving

Understand

What information am I given?
What am I asked to find or do?

Plan

How can I use the information I am given?
Which strategy should I try?

Solve

Did I follow the plan?
Did I show my work?
Did I write the answer?

Check

Did I use the correct information?
Did I do what was asked?
Is my answer reasonable?

Facts	Express each mixed number as an improper fraction.			
$3\frac{1}{3} =$	$1\frac{3}{4} =$	$7\frac{1}{2} =$	$2\frac{2}{3} =$	$2\frac{4}{5} =$
$10\frac{1}{2} =$	$1\frac{7}{8} =$	$33\frac{1}{3} =$	$12\frac{1}{2} =$	$6\frac{2}{3} =$

Express each improper fraction as a mixed number or whole number.

$\frac{8}{4} =$	$\frac{11}{5} =$	$\frac{7}{2} =$	$\frac{14}{3} =$	$\frac{11}{4} =$
$\frac{16}{5} =$	$\frac{24}{6} =$	$\frac{23}{10} =$	$\frac{19}{6} =$	$\frac{16}{7} =$

Mental Math			
a.	**b.**	**c.**	**d.**
e.	**f.**	**g.**	**h.**

Problem Solving

Understand

What information am I given?
What am I asked to find or do?

- -

Plan

How can I use the information I am given?
Which strategy should I try?

- -

Solve

Did I follow the plan?
Did I show my work?
Did I write the answer?

- -

Check

Did I use the correct information?
Did I do what was asked?
Is my answer reasonable?

| Facts | Express each mixed number as an improper fraction. |

$3\frac{1}{3} =$	$1\frac{3}{4} =$	$7\frac{1}{2} =$	$2\frac{2}{3} =$	$2\frac{4}{5} =$
$10\frac{1}{2} =$	$1\frac{7}{8} =$	$33\frac{1}{3} =$	$12\frac{1}{2} =$	$6\frac{2}{3} =$

Express each improper fraction as a mixed number or whole number.

$\frac{8}{4} =$	$\frac{11}{5} =$	$\frac{7}{2} =$	$\frac{14}{3} =$	$\frac{11}{4} =$
$\frac{16}{5} =$	$\frac{24}{6} =$	$\frac{23}{10} =$	$\frac{19}{6} =$	$\frac{16}{7} =$

| Mental Math |

a.	b.	c.	d.
e.	f.	g.	h.

| Problem Solving |

Understand

What information am I given?
What am I asked to find or do?

- -

Plan

How can I use the information I am given?
Which strategy should I try?

- -

Solve

Did I follow the plan?
Did I show my work?
Did I write the answer?

- -

Check

Did I use the correct information?
Did I do what was asked?
Is my answer reasonable?

Facts Simplify. Find the exponent.

$10^3 \cdot 10^4 = 10^{\square}$	$\dfrac{10^6}{10^2} = 10^{\square}$	$(10^3)^2 = 10^{\square}$	$\sqrt{10^2} = 10^{\square}$
$10^{\square} = 1$	$\dfrac{x^4 \cdot x^5}{x^3} = x^{\square}$	$x^4 \cdot x = x^{\square}$	$\dfrac{x^6}{x} = x^{\square}$
$\dfrac{x^3 \cdot x^5}{x^2 \cdot x^4} = x^{\square}$	$(x^4)^2 = x^{\square}$	$(2x^2)^3 = 8x^{\square}$	$\dfrac{x^3}{x^2} = x^{\square}$

Mental Math

a.	**b.**	**c.**	**d.**
e.	**f.**	**g.**	**h.**

Problem Solving

Understand
What information am I given?
What am I asked to find or do?

Plan
How can I use the information I am given?
Which strategy should I try?

Solve
Did I follow the plan?
Did I show my work?
Did I write the answer?

Check
Did I use the correct information?
Did I do what was asked?
Is my answer reasonable?

Facts — Simplify. Find the exponent.

$10^3 \cdot 10^4 = 10^{\square}$	$\dfrac{10^6}{10^2} = 10^{\square}$	$(10^3)^2 = 10^{\square}$	$\sqrt{10^2} = 10^{\square}$
$10^{\square} = 1$	$\dfrac{x^4 \cdot x^5}{x^3} = x^{\square}$	$x^4 \cdot x = x^{\square}$	$\dfrac{x^6}{x} = x^{\square}$
$\dfrac{x^3 \cdot x^5}{x^2 \cdot x^4} = x^{\square}$	$(x^4)^2 = x^{\square}$	$(2x^2)^3 = 8x^{\square}$	$\dfrac{x^3}{x^2} = x^{\square}$

Mental Math

a.	b.	c.	d.
e.	f.	g.	h.

Problem Solving

Understand
What information am I given?
What am I asked to find or do?

Plan
How can I use the information I am given?
Which strategy should I try?

Solve
Did I follow the plan?
Did I show my work?
Did I write the answer?

Check
Did I use the correct information?
Did I do what was asked?
Is my answer reasonable?

Facts · Simplify. Find the exponent.

$10^3 \cdot 10^4 = 10^{\square}$	$\dfrac{10^6}{10^2} = 10^{\square}$	$(10^3)^2 = 10^{\square}$	$\sqrt{10^2} = 10^{\square}$
$10^{\square} = 1$	$\dfrac{x^4 \cdot x^5}{x^3} = x^{\square}$	$x^4 \cdot x = x^{\square}$	$\dfrac{x^6}{X} = x^{\square}$
$\dfrac{x^3 \cdot x^5}{x^2 \cdot x^4} = x^{\square}$	$(x^4)^2 = x^{\square}$	$(2x^2)^3 = 8x^{\square}$	$\dfrac{x^3}{x^2} = x^{\square}$

Mental Math

a.	**b.**	**c.**	**d.**
e.	**f.**	**g.**	**h.**

Problem Solving

Understand
What information am I given?
What am I asked to find or do?

- -

Plan
How can I use the information I am given?
Which strategy should I try?

- -

Solve
Did I follow the plan?
Did I show my work?
Did I write the answer?

- -

Check
Did I use the correct information?
Did I do what was asked?
Is my answer reasonable?

Facts Simplify. Find the exponent.

$10^3 \cdot 10^4 = 10^{\square}$	$\dfrac{10^6}{10^2} = 10^{\square}$	$(10^3)^2 = 10^{\square}$	$\sqrt{10^2} = 10^{\square}$
$10^{\square} = 1$	$\dfrac{x^4 \cdot x^5}{x^3} = x^{\square}$	$x^4 \cdot x = x^{\square}$	$\dfrac{x^6}{x} = x^{\square}$
$\dfrac{x^3 \cdot x^5}{x^2 \cdot x^4} = x^{\square}$	$(x^4)^2 = x^{\square}$	$(2x^2)^3 = 8x^{\square}$	$\dfrac{x^3}{x^2} = x^{\square}$

Mental Math

a.	b.	c.	d.
e.	f.	g.	h.

Problem Solving

Understand

What information am I given?
What am I asked to find or do?

- -

Plan

How can I use the information I am given?
Which strategy should I try?

- -

Solve

Did I follow the plan?
Did I show my work?
Did I write the answer?

- -

Check

Did I use the correct information?
Did I do what was asked?
Is my answer reasonable?

Facts Simplify. Find the exponent.

$10^3 \cdot 10^4 = 10^{\square}$	$\dfrac{10^6}{10^2} = 10^{\square}$	$(10^3)^2 = 10^{\square}$	$\sqrt{10^2} = 10^{\square}$
$10^{\square} = 1$	$\dfrac{x^4 \cdot x^5}{x^3} = x^{\square}$	$x^4 \cdot x = x^{\square}$	$\dfrac{x^6}{x} = x^{\square}$
$\dfrac{x^3 \cdot x^5}{x^2 \cdot x^4} = x^{\square}$	$(x^4)^2 = x^{\square}$	$(2x^2)^3 = 8x^{\square}$	$\dfrac{x^3}{x^2} = x^{\square}$

Mental Math

a.	b.	c.	d.
e.	f.	g.	h.

Problem Solving

Understand

What information am I given?

What am I asked to find or do?

- -

Plan

How can I use the information I am given?

Which strategy should I try?

- -

Solve

Did I follow the plan?

Did I show my work?

Did I write the answer?

- -

Check

Did I use the correct information?

Did I do what was asked?

Is my answer reasonable?

Facts | Express each fraction as a decimal number.

$\frac{1}{5} =$	$\frac{1}{10} =$	$\frac{1}{4} =$	$\frac{1}{20} =$	$\frac{4}{5} =$
$\frac{1}{100} =$	$\frac{1}{2} =$	$\frac{3}{5} =$	$\frac{3}{4} =$	$\frac{9}{10} =$
$\frac{1}{3} =$	$\frac{3}{10} =$	$\frac{1}{6} =$	$\frac{1}{25} =$	$\frac{1}{8} =$
$\frac{1}{9} =$	$\frac{2}{3} =$	$\frac{1}{50} =$	$\frac{2}{5} =$	$\frac{3}{8} =$

Mental Math

a.	b.	c.	d.
e.	f.	g.	h.

Problem Solving

Understand

What information am I given?
What am I asked to find or do?

- -

Plan

How can I use the information I am given?
Which strategy should I try?

- -

Solve

Did I follow the plan?
Did I show my work?
Did I write the answer?

- -

Check

Did I use the correct information?
Did I do what was asked?
Is my answer reasonable?

Facts	Express each fraction as a decimal number.			
$\frac{1}{5} =$	$\frac{1}{10} =$	$\frac{1}{4} =$	$\frac{1}{20} =$	$\frac{4}{5} =$
$\frac{1}{100} =$	$\frac{1}{2} =$	$\frac{3}{5} =$	$\frac{3}{4} =$	$\frac{9}{10} =$
$\frac{1}{3} =$	$\frac{3}{10} =$	$\frac{1}{6} =$	$\frac{1}{25} =$	$\frac{1}{8} =$
$\frac{1}{9} =$	$\frac{2}{3} =$	$\frac{1}{50} =$	$\frac{2}{5} =$	$\frac{3}{8} =$

Mental Math

a.	b.	c.	d.
e.	f.	g.	h.

Problem Solving

Understand

What information am I given?

What am I asked to find or do?

- -

Plan

How can I use the information I am given?

Which strategy should I try?

- -

Solve

Did I follow the plan?

Did I show my work?

Did I write the answer?

- -

Check

Did I use the correct information?

Did I do what was asked?

Is my answer reasonable?

Facts	Express each fraction as a decimal number.			
$\frac{1}{5} =$	$\frac{1}{10} =$	$\frac{1}{4} =$	$\frac{1}{20} =$	$\frac{4}{5} =$
$\frac{1}{100} =$	$\frac{1}{2} =$	$\frac{3}{5} =$	$\frac{3}{4} =$	$\frac{9}{10} =$
$\frac{1}{3} =$	$\frac{3}{10} =$	$\frac{1}{6} =$	$\frac{1}{25} =$	$\frac{1}{8} =$
$\frac{1}{9} =$	$\frac{2}{3} =$	$\frac{1}{50} =$	$\frac{2}{5} =$	$\frac{3}{8} =$

Mental Math

a.	**b.**	**c.**	**d.**
e.	**f.**	**g.**	**h.**

Problem Solving

Understand

What information am I given?
What am I asked to find or do?

Plan

How can I use the information I am given?
Which strategy should I try?

Solve

Did I follow the plan?
Did I show my work?
Did I write the answer?

Check

Did I use the correct information?
Did I do what was asked?
Is my answer reasonable?

Facts   Express each fraction as a decimal number.

$\frac{1}{5} =$	$\frac{1}{10} =$	$\frac{1}{4} =$	$\frac{1}{20} =$	$\frac{4}{5} =$
$\frac{1}{100} =$	$\frac{1}{2} =$	$\frac{3}{5} =$	$\frac{3}{4} =$	$\frac{9}{10} =$
$\frac{1}{3} =$	$\frac{3}{10} =$	$\frac{1}{6} =$	$\frac{1}{25} =$	$\frac{1}{8} =$
$\frac{1}{9} =$	$\frac{2}{3} =$	$\frac{1}{50} =$	$\frac{2}{5} =$	$\frac{3}{8} =$

Mental Math

a.	**b.**	**c.**	**d.**
e.	**f.**	**g.**	**h.**

Problem Solving

Understand

What information am I given?
What am I asked to find or do?

Plan

How can I use the information I am given?
Which strategy should I try?

Solve

Did I follow the plan?
Did I show my work?
Did I write the answer?

Check

Did I use the correct information?
Did I do what was asked?
Is my answer reasonable?

Facts — Express each fraction as a decimal number.

$\frac{1}{5}$ =	$\frac{1}{10}$ =	$\frac{1}{4}$ =	$\frac{1}{20}$ =	$\frac{4}{5}$ =
$\frac{1}{100}$ =	$\frac{1}{2}$ =	$\frac{3}{5}$ =	$\frac{3}{4}$ =	$\frac{9}{10}$ =
$\frac{1}{3}$ =	$\frac{3}{10}$ =	$\frac{1}{6}$ =	$\frac{1}{25}$ =	$\frac{1}{8}$ =
$\frac{1}{9}$ =	$\frac{2}{3}$ =	$\frac{1}{50}$ =	$\frac{2}{5}$ =	$\frac{3}{8}$ =

Mental Math

a.	**b.**	**c.**	**d.**
e.	**f.**	**g.**	**h.**

Problem Solving

Understand

What information am I given?

What am I asked to find or do?

Plan

How can I use the information I am given?

Which strategy should I try?

Solve

Did I follow the plan?

Did I show my work?

Did I write the answer?

Check

Did I use the correct information?

Did I do what was asked?

Is my answer reasonable?

Facts	Simplify.		
$(-3) + (-5)$	$(-3) - (-5)$	$(-3)(-5)$	$\dfrac{-30}{-5}$
$(-8) + (+2)$	$(-8) - (+2)$	$(-8)(+2)$	$\dfrac{-8}{+2}$
$-3 + -2 - -4$	$-5 - +6 + +2$	$(-3)(+2)(-6)$	$\dfrac{(-2)(-6)}{-3}$

Mental Math

a.	b.	c.	d.
e.	f.	g.	h.

Problem Solving

Understand

What information am I given?

What am I asked to find or do?

- -

Plan

How can I use the information I am given?

Which strategy should I try?

- -

Solve

Did I follow the plan?

Did I show my work?

Did I write the answer?

- -

Check

Did I use the correct information?

Did I do what was asked?

Is my answer reasonable?

Facts   Simplify.

$(-3) + (-5)$	$(-3) - (-5)$	$(-3)(-5)$	$\dfrac{-30}{-5}$
$(-8) + (+2)$	$(-8) - (+2)$	$(-8)(+2)$	$\dfrac{-8}{+2}$
$-3 + -2 - -4$	$-5 - +6 + +2$	$(-3)(+2)(-6)$	$\dfrac{(-2)(-6)}{-3}$

Mental Math

a.	b.	c.	d.
e.	f.	g.	h.

Problem Solving

Understand

What information am I given?
What am I asked to find or do?

- -

Plan

How can I use the information I am given?
Which strategy should I try?

- -

Solve

Did I follow the plan?
Did I show my work?
Did I write the answer?

- -

Check

Did I use the correct information?
Did I do what was asked?
Is my answer reasonable?

Facts   Simplify.

$(-3) + (-5)$	$(-3) - (-5)$	$(-3)(-5)$	$\dfrac{-30}{-5}$
$(-8) + (+2)$	$(-8) - (+2)$	$(-8)(+2)$	$\dfrac{-8}{+2}$
$-3 + -2 - -4$	$-5 - +6 + +2$	$(-3)(+2)(-6)$	$\dfrac{(-2)(-6)}{-3}$

Mental Math

a.	**b.**	**c.**	**d.**
e.	**f.**	**g.**	**h.**

Problem Solving

Understand

What information am I given?
What am I asked to find or do?

Plan

How can I use the information I am given?
Which strategy should I try?

Solve

Did I follow the plan?
Did I show my work?
Did I write the answer?

Check

Did I use the correct information?
Did I do what was asked?
Is my answer reasonable?

Name _____ Time _____

Power Up ☐ I

Use with **Lesson 44**

Facts   Simplify.

$(-3) + (-5)$	$(-3) - (-5)$	$(-3)(-5)$	$\dfrac{-30}{-5}$
$(-8) + (+2)$	$(-8) - (+2)$	$(-8)(+2)$	$\dfrac{-8}{+2}$
$-3 + -2 - -4$	$-5 - +6 + +2$	$(-3)(+2)(-6)$	$\dfrac{(-2)(-6)}{-3}$

Mental Math

a.	b.	c.	d.
e.	f.	g.	h.

Problem Solving

Understand
What information am I given?
What am I asked to find or do?

- -

Plan
How can I use the information I am given?
Which strategy should I try?

- -

Solve
Did I follow the plan?
Did I show my work?
Did I write the answer?

- -

Check
Did I use the correct information?
Did I do what was asked?
Is my answer reasonable?

© Houghton Mifflin Harcourt Publishing Company and Stephen Hake

44

Saxon Math Course 3

Facts   Simplify.

$(-3) + (-5)$	$(-3) - (-5)$	$(-3)(-5)$	$\dfrac{-30}{-5}$
$(-8) + (+2)$	$(-8) - (+2)$	$(-8)(+2)$	$\dfrac{-8}{+2}$
$-3 + -2 - -4$	$-5 - +6 + +2$	$(-3)(+2)(-6)$	$\dfrac{(-2)(-6)}{-3}$

Mental Math

a.	**b.**	**c.**	**d.**
e.	**f.**	**g.**	**h.**

Problem Solving

Understand
What information am I given?
What am I asked to find or do?

Plan
How can I use the information I am given?
Which strategy should I try?

Solve
Did I follow the plan?
Did I show my work?
Did I write the answer?

Check
Did I use the correct information?
Did I do what was asked?
Is my answer reasonable?

Facts   Write the word that completes each sentence.

1. The distance around a circle is its _____.

2. Every point on a circle is the same distance from the _____.

3. The distance across a circle through its center is its _____.

4. The distance from a circle to its center is its _____.

5. Two or more circles with the same center are _____ circles.

6. A segment between two points on a circle is a _____.

7. Part of a circumference is an _____.

8. A portion of a circle and its interior, bound by an arc and two radii, is a _____.

9. Half of a circle is a _____.

10. An angle whose vertex is the center of a circle is a _____ angle.

Mental Math

a.	b.	c.	d.
e.	f.	g.	h.

Problem Solving

Understand

What information am I given?
What am I asked to find or do?

- -

Plan

How can I use the information I am given?
Which strategy should I try?

- -

Solve

Did I follow the plan?
Did I show my work?
Did I write the answer?

- -

Check

Did I use the correct information?
Did I do what was asked?
Is my answer reasonable?

Saxon Math Course 3

Facts   Write the word that completes each sentence.

1. The distance around a circle is its _____.

2. Every point on a circle is the same distance from the _____.

3. The distance across a circle through its center is its _____.

4. The distance from a circle to its center is its _____.

5. Two or more circles with the same center are _____ circles.

6. A segment between two points on a circle is a _____.

7. Part of a circumference is an _____.

8. A portion of a circle and its interior, bound by an arc and two radii, is a _____.

9. Half of a circle is a _____.

10. An angle whose vertex is the center of a circle is a _____ angle.

Mental Math

a.	b.	c.	d.
e.	f.	g.	h.

Problem Solving

Understand
What information am I given?
What am I asked to find or do?

Plan
How can I use the information I am given?
Which strategy should I try?

Solve
Did I follow the plan?
Did I show my work?
Did I write the answer?

Check
Did I use the correct information?
Did I do what was asked?
Is my answer reasonable?

Facts   Write the word that completes each sentence.

1. The distance around a circle is its _____.

2. Every point on a circle is the same distance from the _____.

3. The distance across a circle through its center is its _____.

4. The distance from a circle to its center is its _____.

5. Two or more circles with the same center are _____ circles.

6. A segment between two points on a circle is a _____.

7. Part of a circumference is an _____.

8. A portion of a circle and its interior, bound by an arc and two radii, is a _____.

9. Half of a circle is a _____.

10. An angle whose vertex is the center of a circle is a _____ angle.

Mental Math

a.	b.	c.	d.
e.	f.	g.	h.

Problem Solving

Understand
What information am I given?
What am I asked to find or do?

Plan
How can I use the information I am given?
Which strategy should I try?

Solve
Did I follow the plan?
Did I show my work?
Did I write the answer?

Check
Did I use the correct information?
Did I do what was asked?
Is my answer reasonable?

Facts   Write the word that completes each sentence.

1. The distance around a circle is its _____.

2. Every point on a circle is the same distance from the _____.

3. The distance across a circle through its center is its _____.

4. The distance from a circle to its center is its _____.

5. Two or more circles with the same center are _____ circles.

6. A segment between two points on a circle is a _____.

7. Part of a circumference is an _____.

8. A portion of a circle and its interior, bound by an arc and two radii, is a _____.

9. Half of a circle is a _____.

10. An angle whose vertex is the center of a circle is a _____ angle.

Mental Math

a.	b.	c.	d.
e.	f.	g.	h.

Problem Solving

Understand
What information am I given?
What am I asked to find or do?

- -

Plan
How can I use the information I am given?
Which strategy should I try?

- -

Solve
Did I follow the plan?
Did I show my work?
Did I write the answer?

- -

Check
Did I use the correct information?
Did I do what was asked?
Is my answer reasonable?

Facts · Write the word that completes each sentence.

1. The distance around a circle is its _____.

2. Every point on a circle is the same distance from the _____.

3. The distance across a circle through its center is its _____.

4. The distance from a circle to its center is its _____.

5. Two or more circles with the same center are _____ circles.

6. A segment between two points on a circle is a _____.

7. Part of a circumference is an _____.

8. A portion of a circle and its interior, bound by an arc and two radii, is a _____.

9. Half of a circle is a _____.

10. An angle whose vertex is the center of a circle is a _____ angle.

Mental Math

a.	b.	c.	d.
e.	f.	g.	h.

Problem Solving

Understand

What information am I given?
What am I asked to find or do?

- -

Plan

How can I use the information I am given?
Which strategy should I try?

- -

Solve

Did I follow the plan?
Did I show my work?
Did I write the answer?

- -

Check

Did I use the correct information?
Did I do what was asked?
Is my answer reasonable?

Facts   Find the value of each variable.

$a + 8 = 20$ $a =$	$b - 6 = 18$ $b =$	$3c = 24$ $c =$	$\dfrac{d}{4} = 8$ $d =$	$x^2 = 25$ $x =$
$7 + e = 15$ $e =$	$20 - f = 5$ $f =$	$(g)(4) = 20$ $g =$	$\dfrac{12}{h} = 6$ $h =$	$\sqrt{w} = 4$ $w =$
$18 = j + 11$ $j =$	$17 = k - 4$ $k =$	$24 = 6m$ $m =$	$6 = \dfrac{n}{3}$ $n =$	$\lvert z \rvert = 3$ $z =$
$14 = 5 + q$ $q =$	$30 = 40 - r$ $r =$	$32 = (s)(4)$ $s =$	$8 = \dfrac{24}{t}$ $t =$	$\dfrac{1}{2}y = 8$ $y =$

Mental Math

a.	**b.**	**c.**	**d.**
e.	**f.**	**g.**	**h.**

Problem Solving

Understand

What information am I given?
What am I asked to find or do?

- -

Plan

How can I use the information I am given?
Which strategy should I try?

- -

Solve

Did I follow the plan?
Did I show my work?
Did I write the answer?

- -

Check

Did I use the correct information?
Did I do what was asked?
Is my answer reasonable?

© Houghton Mifflin Harcourt Publishing Company and Stephen Hake

Facts   Find the value of each variable.

$a + 8 = 20$	$b - 6 = 18$	$3c = 24$	$\dfrac{d}{4} = 8$	$x^2 = 25$
$a =$	$b =$	$c =$	$d =$	$x =$
$7 + e = 15$	$20 - f = 5$	$(g)(4) = 20$	$\dfrac{12}{h} = 6$	$\sqrt{w} = 4$
$e =$	$f =$	$g =$	$h =$	$w =$
$18 = j + 11$	$17 = k - 4$	$24 = 6m$	$6 = \dfrac{n}{3}$	$|z| = 3$
$j =$	$k =$	$m =$	$n =$	$z =$
$14 = 5 + q$	$30 = 40 - r$	$32 = (s)(4)$	$8 = \dfrac{24}{t}$	$\dfrac{1}{2}y = 8$
$q =$	$r =$	$s =$	$t =$	$y =$

Mental Math

a.	b.	c.	d.
e.	f.	g.	h.

Problem Solving

Understand
What information am I given?
What am I asked to find or do?

- -

Plan
How can I use the information I am given?
Which strategy should I try?

- -

Solve
Did I follow the plan?
Did I show my work?
Did I write the answer?

- -

Check
Did I use the correct information?
Did I do what was asked?
Is my answer reasonable?

| **Facts** | Find the value of each variable. | | | |

$a + 8 = 20$	$b - 6 = 18$	$3c = 24$	$\dfrac{d}{4} = 8$	$x^2 = 25$
$a =$	$b =$	$c =$	$d =$	$x =$
$7 + e = 15$	$20 - f = 5$	$(g)(4) = 20$	$\dfrac{12}{h} = 6$	$\sqrt{w} = 4$
$e =$	$f =$	$g =$	$h =$	$w =$
$18 = j + 11$	$17 = k - 4$	$24 = 6m$	$6 = \dfrac{n}{3}$	$|z| = 3$
$j =$	$k =$	$m =$	$n =$	$z =$
$14 = 5 + q$	$30 = 40 - r$	$32 = (s)(4)$	$8 = \dfrac{24}{t}$	$\dfrac{1}{2}y = 8$
$q =$	$r =$	$s =$	$t =$	$y =$

Mental Math			
a.	**b.**	**c.**	**d.**
e.	**f.**	**g.**	**h.**

Problem Solving

Understand

What information am I given?
What am I asked to find or do?

- -

Plan

How can I use the information I am given?
Which strategy should I try?

- -

Solve

Did I follow the plan?
Did I show my work?
Did I write the answer?

- -

Check

Did I use the correct information?
Did I do what was asked?
Is my answer reasonable?

| Facts | Find the value of each variable. | | | |

$a + 8 = 20$ $a =$	$b - 6 = 18$ $b =$	$3c = 24$ $c =$	$\dfrac{d}{4} = 8$ $d =$	$x^2 = 25$ $x =$
$7 + e = 15$ $e =$	$20 - f = 5$ $f =$	$(g)(4) = 20$ $g =$	$\dfrac{12}{h} = 6$ $h =$	$\sqrt{w} = 4$ $w =$
$18 = j + 11$ $j =$	$17 = k - 4$ $k =$	$24 = 6m$ $m =$	$6 = \dfrac{n}{3}$ $n =$	$|z| = 3$ $z =$
$14 = 5 + q$ $q =$	$30 = 40 - r$ $r =$	$32 = (s)(4)$ $s =$	$8 = \dfrac{24}{t}$ $t =$	$\dfrac{1}{2}y = 8$ $y =$

Mental Math

a.	b.	c.	d.
e.	f.	g.	h.

Problem Solving

Understand

What information am I given?
What am I asked to find or do?

- -

Plan

How can I use the information I am given?
Which strategy should I try?

- -

Solve

Did I follow the plan?
Did I show my work?
Did I write the answer?

- -

Check

Did I use the correct information?
Did I do what was asked?
Is my answer reasonable?

Facts   Find the value of each variable.

$a + 8 = 20$	$b - 6 = 18$	$3c = 24$	$\dfrac{d}{4} = 8$	$x^2 = 25$
$a =$	$b =$	$c =$	$d =$	$x =$
$7 + e = 15$	$20 - f = 5$	$(g)(4) = 20$	$\dfrac{12}{h} = 6$	$\sqrt{w} = 4$
$e =$	$f =$	$g =$	$h =$	$w =$
$18 = j + 11$	$17 = k - 4$	$24 = 6m$	$6 = \dfrac{n}{3}$	$|z| = 3$
$j =$	$k =$	$m =$	$n =$	$z =$
$14 = 5 + q$	$30 = 40 - r$	$32 = (s)(4)$	$8 = \dfrac{24}{t}$	$\dfrac{1}{2}y = 8$
$q =$	$r =$	$s =$	$t =$	$y =$

Mental Math

a.	b.	c.	d.
e.	f.	g.	h.

Problem Solving

Understand

What information am I given?

What am I asked to find or do?

- -

Plan

How can I use the information I am given?

Which strategy should I try?

- -

Solve

Did I follow the plan?

Did I show my work?

Did I write the answer?

- -

Check

Did I use the correct information?

Did I do what was asked?

Is my answer reasonable?

Facts	Write each number in scientific notation.	
	186,000 =	0.0002 =
	2,050,000 =	$\frac{1}{1,000,000}$ =
	15 million =	12 thousandths =

Write each number in standard form.

3×10^5 =	1×10^{-3} =
3.75×10^4 =	3.5×10^{-5} =
4.05×10^3 =	2.04×10^{-2} =

Mental Math			
a.	**b.**	**c.**	**d.**
e.	**f.**	**g.**	**h.**

Problem Solving

Understand
What information am I given?
What am I asked to find or do?

Plan
How can I use the information I am given?
Which strategy should I try?

Solve
Did I follow the plan?
Did I show my work?
Did I write the answer?

Check
Did I use the correct information?
Did I do what was asked?
Is my answer reasonable?

Facts	Write each number in scientific notation.
186,000 =	0.0002 =
2,050,000 =	$\dfrac{1}{1,000,000}$ =
15 million =	12 thousandths =

Write each number in standard form.

3×10^5 =	1×10^{-3} =
3.75×10^4 =	3.5×10^{-5} =
4.05×10^3 =	2.04×10^{-2} =

Mental Math

a.	b.	c.	d.
e.	f.	g.	h.

Problem Solving

Understand

What information am I given?
What am I asked to find or do?

- -

Plan

How can I use the information I am given?
Which strategy should I try?

- -

Solve

Did I follow the plan?
Did I show my work?
Did I write the answer?

- -

Check

Did I use the correct information?
Did I do what was asked?
Is my answer reasonable?

Facts	Write each number in scientific notation.	
186,000 =	0.0002 =
2,050,000 =	$\dfrac{1}{1,000,000}$ =
15 million =	12 thousandths =

Write each number in standard form.

3×10^5 =	1×10^{-3} =
3.75×10^4 =	3.5×10^{-5} =
4.05×10^3 =	2.04×10^{-2} =

Mental Math

a.	b.	c.	d.
e.	f.	g.	h.

Problem Solving

Understand
What information am I given?
What am I asked to find or do?

Plan
How can I use the information I am given?
Which strategy should I try?

Solve
Did I follow the plan?
Did I show my work?
Did I write the answer?

Check
Did I use the correct information?
Did I do what was asked?
Is my answer reasonable?

Saxon Math Course 3

Facts   Write each number in scientific notation.

186,000 =	0.0002 =
2,050,000 =	$\dfrac{1}{1,000,000}$ =
15 million =	12 thousandths =

Write each number in standard form.

3×10^5 =	1×10^{-3} =
3.75×10^4 =	3.5×10^{-5} =
4.05×10^3 =	2.04×10^{-2} =

Mental Math

a.	b.	c.	d.
e.	f.	g.	h.

Problem Solving

Understand
What information am I given?
What am I asked to find or do?

- -

Plan
How can I use the information I am given?
Which strategy should I try?

- -

Solve
Did I follow the plan?
Did I show my work?
Did I write the answer?

- -

Check
Did I use the correct information?
Did I do what was asked?
Is my answer reasonable?

Facts	Write each number in scientific notation.	
186,000 =	0.0002 =
2,050,000 =	$\frac{1}{1,000,000}$ =
15 million =	12 thousandths =

Write each number in standard form.

3×10^5 =	1×10^{-3} =
3.75×10^4 =	3.5×10^{-5} =
4.05×10^3 =	2.04×10^{-2} =

Mental Math			
a.	**b.**	**c.**	**d.**
e.	**f.**	**g.**	**h.**

Problem Solving

Understand

What information am I given?
What am I asked to find or do?

- -

Plan

How can I use the information I am given?
Which strategy should I try?

- -

Solve

Did I follow the plan?
Did I show my work?
Did I write the answer?

- -

Check

Did I use the correct information?
Did I do what was asked?
Is my answer reasonable?

Saxon Math Course 3

Facts Express each percent as a reduced fraction.

1% =	100% =	50% =	70% =	20% =
150% =	$66\frac{2}{3}$% =	5% =	$12\frac{1}{2}$% =	90% =
25% =	2% =	10% =	$33\frac{1}{3}$% =	4% =
40% =	$16\frac{2}{3}$% =	75% =	30% =	80% =

Mental Math

a.	b.	c.	d.
e.	f.	g.	h.

Problem Solving

Understand

What information am I given?
What am I asked to find or do?

- -

Plan

How can I use the information I am given?
Which strategy should I try?

- -

Solve

Did I follow the plan?
Did I show my work?
Did I write the answer?

- -

Check

Did I use the correct information?
Did I do what was asked?
Is my answer reasonable?

Facts   Express each percent as a reduced fraction.

1% =	100% =	50% =	70% =	20% =
150% =	$66\frac{2}{3}$% =	5% =	$12\frac{1}{2}$% =	90% =
25% =	2% =	10% =	$33\frac{1}{3}$% =	4% =
40% =	$16\frac{2}{3}$% =	75% =	30% =	80% =

Mental Math

a.	**b.**	**c.**	**d.**
e.	**f.**	**g.**	**h.**

Problem Solving

Understand

What information am I given?
What am I asked to find or do?

- -

Plan

How can I use the information I am given?
Which strategy should I try?

- -

Solve

Did I follow the plan?
Did I show my work?
Did I write the answer?

- -

Check

Did I use the correct information?
Did I do what was asked?
Is my answer reasonable?

Facts   Express each percent as a reduced fraction.

1% =	100% =	50% =	70% =	20% =
150% =	$66\frac{2}{3}$% =	5% =	$12\frac{1}{2}$% =	90% =
25% =	2% =	10% =	$33\frac{1}{3}$% =	4% =
40% =	$16\frac{2}{3}$% =	75% =	30% =	80% =

Mental Math

a.	b.	c.	d.
e.	f.	g.	h.

Problem Solving

Understand

What information am I given?

What am I asked to find or do?

- -

Plan

How can I use the information I am given?

Which strategy should I try?

- -

Solve

Did I follow the plan?

Did I show my work?

Did I write the answer?

- -

Check

Did I use the correct information?

Did I do what was asked?

Is my answer reasonable?

Facts   Express each percent as a reduced fraction.

1% =	100% =	50% =	70% =	20% =
150% =	$66\frac{2}{3}$% =	5% =	$12\frac{1}{2}$% =	90% =
25% =	2% =	10% =	$33\frac{1}{3}$% =	4% =
40% =	$16\frac{2}{3}$% =	75% =	30% =	80% =

Mental Math

a.	b.	c.	d.
e.	f.	g.	h.

Problem Solving

Understand
What information am I given?
What am I asked to find or do?

- -

Plan
How can I use the information I am given?
Which strategy should I try?

- -

Solve
Did I follow the plan?
Did I show my work?
Did I write the answer?

- -

Check
Did I use the correct information?
Did I do what was asked?
Is my answer reasonable?

Facts Express each percent as a reduced fraction.

1% =	100% =	50% =	70% =	20% =
150% =	$66\frac{2}{3}$% =	5% =	$12\frac{1}{2}$% =	90% =
25% =	2% =	10% =	$33\frac{1}{3}$% =	4% =
40% =	$16\frac{2}{3}$% =	75% =	30% =	80% =

Mental Math

a.	b.	c.	d.
e.	f.	g.	h.

Problem Solving

Understand
What information am I given?
What am I asked to find or do?

Plan
How can I use the information I am given?
Which strategy should I try?

Solve
Did I follow the plan?
Did I show my work?
Did I write the answer?

Check
Did I use the correct information?
Did I do what was asked?
Is my answer reasonable?

Facts   Solve each proportion.

$\dfrac{x}{12} = \dfrac{4}{6}$	$\dfrac{5}{x} = \dfrac{10}{30}$	$\dfrac{8}{16} = \dfrac{x}{4}$	$\dfrac{3}{6} = \dfrac{9}{x}$
$x =$	$x =$	$x =$	$x =$
$\dfrac{x}{20} = \dfrac{2}{10}$	$\dfrac{3}{x} = \dfrac{5}{15}$	$\dfrac{7}{14} = \dfrac{x}{12}$	$\dfrac{3}{12} = \dfrac{5}{x}$
$x =$	$x =$	$x =$	$x =$
$\dfrac{x}{100} = \dfrac{5}{25}$	$\dfrac{12}{x} = \dfrac{60}{20}$	$\dfrac{10}{100} = \dfrac{x}{50}$	$\dfrac{9}{27} = \dfrac{10}{x}$
$x =$	$x =$	$x =$	$x =$

Mental Math

a.	b.	c.	d.
e.	f.	g.	h.

Problem Solving

Understand
What information am I given?
What am I asked to find or do?

Plan
How can I use the information I am given?
Which strategy should I try?

Solve
Did I follow the plan?
Did I show my work?
Did I write the answer?

Check
Did I use the correct information?
Did I do what was asked?
Is my answer reasonable?

Facts	Solve each proportion.		
$\dfrac{x}{12} = \dfrac{4}{6}$ $x =$	$\dfrac{5}{x} = \dfrac{10}{30}$ $x =$	$\dfrac{8}{16} = \dfrac{x}{4}$ $x =$	$\dfrac{3}{6} = \dfrac{9}{x}$ $x =$
$\dfrac{x}{20} = \dfrac{2}{10}$ $x =$	$\dfrac{3}{x} = \dfrac{5}{15}$ $x =$	$\dfrac{7}{14} = \dfrac{x}{12}$ $x =$	$\dfrac{3}{12} = \dfrac{5}{x}$ $x =$
$\dfrac{x}{100} = \dfrac{5}{25}$ $x =$	$\dfrac{12}{x} = \dfrac{60}{20}$ $x =$	$\dfrac{10}{100} = \dfrac{x}{50}$ $x =$	$\dfrac{9}{27} = \dfrac{10}{x}$ $x =$

Mental Math			
a.	**b.**	**c.**	**d.**
e.	**f.**	**g.**	**h.**

Problem Solving

Understand

What information am I given?
What am I asked to find or do?

- -

Plan

How can I use the information I am given?
Which strategy should I try?

- -

Solve

Did I follow the plan?
Did I show my work?
Did I write the answer?

- -

Check

Did I use the correct information?
Did I do what was asked?
Is my answer reasonable?

Facts Solve each proportion.

$\dfrac{x}{12} = \dfrac{4}{6}$ $x =$	$\dfrac{5}{x} = \dfrac{10}{30}$ $x =$	$\dfrac{8}{16} = \dfrac{x}{4}$ $x =$	$\dfrac{3}{6} = \dfrac{9}{x}$ $x =$
$\dfrac{x}{20} = \dfrac{2}{10}$ $x =$	$\dfrac{3}{x} = \dfrac{5}{15}$ $x =$	$\dfrac{7}{14} = \dfrac{x}{12}$ $x =$	$\dfrac{3}{12} = \dfrac{5}{x}$ $x =$
$\dfrac{x}{100} = \dfrac{5}{25}$ $x =$	$\dfrac{12}{x} = \dfrac{60}{20}$ $x =$	$\dfrac{10}{100} = \dfrac{x}{50}$ $x =$	$\dfrac{9}{27} = \dfrac{10}{x}$ $x =$

Mental Math

a.	**b.**	**c.**	**d.**
e.	**f.**	**g.**	**h.**

Problem Solving

Understand

What information am I given?

What am I asked to find or do?

- -

Plan

How can I use the information I am given?

Which strategy should I try?

- -

Solve

Did I follow the plan?

Did I show my work?

Did I write the answer?

- -

Check

Did I use the correct information?

Did I do what was asked?

Is my answer reasonable?

Facts   Solve each proportion.

$\dfrac{x}{12} = \dfrac{4}{6}$	$\dfrac{5}{x} = \dfrac{10}{30}$	$\dfrac{8}{16} = \dfrac{x}{4}$	$\dfrac{3}{6} = \dfrac{9}{x}$
$x =$	$x =$	$x =$	$x =$
$\dfrac{x}{20} = \dfrac{2}{10}$	$\dfrac{3}{x} = \dfrac{5}{15}$	$\dfrac{7}{14} = \dfrac{x}{12}$	$\dfrac{3}{12} = \dfrac{5}{x}$
$x =$	$x =$	$x =$	$x =$
$\dfrac{x}{100} = \dfrac{5}{25}$	$\dfrac{12}{x} = \dfrac{60}{20}$	$\dfrac{10}{100} = \dfrac{x}{50}$	$\dfrac{9}{27} = \dfrac{10}{x}$
$x =$	$x =$	$x =$	$x =$

Mental Math

a.	**b.**	**c.**	**d.**
e.	**f.**	**g.**	**h.**

Problem Solving

Understand

What information am I given?

What am I asked to find or do?

- -

Plan

How can I use the information I am given?

Which strategy should I try?

- -

Solve

Did I follow the plan?

Did I show my work?

Did I write the answer?

- -

Check

Did I use the correct information?

Did I do what was asked?

Is my answer reasonable?

Facts   Solve each proportion.

$\dfrac{x}{12} = \dfrac{4}{6}$	$\dfrac{5}{x} = \dfrac{10}{30}$	$\dfrac{8}{16} = \dfrac{x}{4}$	$\dfrac{3}{6} = \dfrac{9}{x}$
$x =$	$x =$	$x =$	$x =$
$\dfrac{x}{20} = \dfrac{2}{10}$	$\dfrac{3}{x} = \dfrac{5}{15}$	$\dfrac{7}{14} = \dfrac{x}{12}$	$\dfrac{3}{12} = \dfrac{5}{x}$
$x =$	$x =$	$x =$	$x =$
$\dfrac{x}{100} = \dfrac{5}{25}$	$\dfrac{12}{x} = \dfrac{60}{20}$	$\dfrac{10}{100} = \dfrac{x}{50}$	$\dfrac{9}{27} = \dfrac{10}{x}$
$x =$	$x =$	$x =$	$x =$

Mental Math

a.	b.	c.	d.
e.	f.	g.	h.

Problem Solving

Understand

What information am I given?

What am I asked to find or do?

- -

Plan

How can I use the information I am given?

Which strategy should I try?

- -

Solve

Did I follow the plan?

Did I show my work?

Did I write the answer?

- -

Check

Did I use the correct information?

Did I do what was asked?

Is my answer reasonable?

Facts   Find the measure of the angle indicated by the letters.

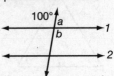

parallel lines 1 and 2

m∠a = _____

m∠b = _____

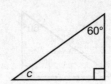

m∠c = _____

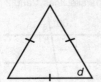

m∠d = _____

m∠f = _____

m∠g = _____

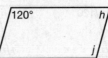

parallelogram

m∠h = _____

m∠j = _____

m∠k = _____

Mental Math

a.	b.	c.	d.
e.	f.	g.	h.

Problem Solving

Understand

What information am I given?
What am I asked to find or do?

Plan

How can I use the information I am given?
Which strategy should I try?

Solve

Did I follow the plan?
Did I show my work?
Did I write the answer?

Check

Did I use the correct information?
Did I do what was asked?
Is my answer reasonable?

Facts   Find the measure of the angle indicated by the letters.

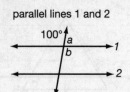

parallel lines 1 and 2

m∠a = _____

m∠b = _____

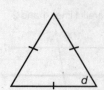

m∠c = _____

m∠d = _____

m∠f = _____

m∠g = _____

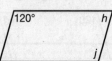

parallelogram

m∠h = _____

m∠j = _____

m∠k = _____

Mental Math

a.	**b.**	**c.**	**d.**
e.	**f.**	**g.**	**h.**

Problem Solving

Understand

What information am I given?
What am I asked to find or do?

Plan

How can I use the information I am given?
Which strategy should I try?

Solve

Did I follow the plan?
Did I show my work?
Did I write the answer?

Check

Did I use the correct information?
Did I do what was asked?
Is my answer reasonable?

Saxon Math Course 3

Facts   Find the measure of the angle indicated by the letters.

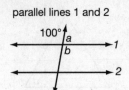

parallel lines 1 and 2

m∠a = _____

m∠b = _____

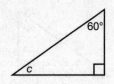

m∠c = _____

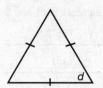

m∠d = _____

m∠f = _____

m∠g = _____

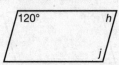

parallelogram

m∠h = _____

m∠j = _____

m∠k = _____

Mental Math

a.	b.	c.	d.
e.	f.	g.	h.

Problem Solving

Understand
What information am I given?
What am I asked to find or do?

- -

Plan
How can I use the information I am given?
Which strategy should I try?

- -

Solve
Did I follow the plan?
Did I show my work?
Did I write the answer?

- -

Check
Did I use the correct information?
Did I do what was asked?
Is my answer reasonable?

Facts Find the measure of the angle indicated by the letters.

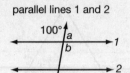

parallel lines 1 and 2

m∠a = _____

m∠b = _____

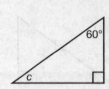

m∠c = _____

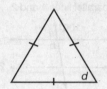

m∠d = _____

m∠f = _____

m∠g = _____

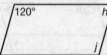

parallelogram

m∠h = _____

m∠j = _____

m∠k = _____

Mental Math

a.	b.	c.	d.
e.	f.	g.	h.

Problem Solving

Understand

What information am I given?

What am I asked to find or do?

Plan

How can I use the information I am given?

Which strategy should I try?

Solve

Did I follow the plan?

Did I show my work?

Did I write the answer?

Check

Did I use the correct information?

Did I do what was asked?

Is my answer reasonable?

Facts   Find the measure of the angle indicated by the letters.

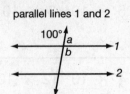

parallel lines 1 and 2

m∠a = _____

m∠b = _____

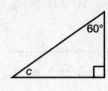

m∠c = _____

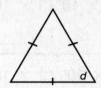

m∠d = _____

m∠f = _____

m∠g = _____

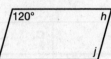

parallelogram

m∠h = _____

m∠j = _____

m∠k = _____

Mental Math

a.	b.	c.	d.
e.	f.	g.	h.

Problem Solving

Understand

What information am I given?

What am I asked to find or do?

- -

Plan

How can I use the information I am given?

Which strategy should I try?

- -

Solve

Did I follow the plan?

Did I show my work?

Did I write the answer?

- -

Check

Did I use the correct information?

Did I do what was asked?

Is my answer reasonable?

Facts — Simplify and express in scientific notation.

$(2 \times 10^6)(3 \times 10^4)$	$(4 \times 10^5)(6 \times 10^4)$	$(2.5 \times 10^3)(3 \times 10^{-6})$
$(4 \times 10^{-3})(2 \times 10^{-4})$	$(5 \times 10^{-5})(3 \times 10^{-4})$	$(2.4 \times 10^{-4})(2 \times 10^6)$

$\dfrac{6 \times 10^8}{3 \times 10^5}$	$\dfrac{5 \times 10^4}{2 \times 10^8}$	$\dfrac{4.2 \times 10^{-3}}{2 \times 10^3}$	$\dfrac{2.4 \times 10^5}{4 \times 10^{-3}}$

Mental Math

a.	**b.**	**c.**	**d.**
e.	**f.**	**g.**	**h.**

Problem Solving

Understand

What information am I given?

What am I asked to find or do?

Plan

How can I use the information I am given?

Which strategy should I try?

Solve

Did I follow the plan?

Did I show my work?

Did I write the answer?

Check

Did I use the correct information?

Did I do what was asked?

Is my answer reasonable?

Facts	Simplify and express in scientific notation.	
$(2 \times 10^6)(3 \times 10^4)$	$(4 \times 10^5)(6 \times 10^4)$	$(2.5 \times 10^3)(3 \times 10^{-6})$
$(4 \times 10^{-3})(2 \times 10^{-4})$	$(5 \times 10^{-5})(3 \times 10^{-4})$	$(2.4 \times 10^{-4})(2 \times 10^6)$

$\dfrac{6 \times 10^8}{3 \times 10^5}$	$\dfrac{5 \times 10^4}{2 \times 10^8}$	$\dfrac{4.2 \times 10^{-3}}{2 \times 10^3}$	$\dfrac{2.4 \times 10^5}{4 \times 10^{-3}}$

Mental Math			
a.	b.	c.	d.
e.	f.	g.	h.

Problem Solving

Understand
What information am I given?
What am I asked to find or do?

Plan
How can I use the information I am given?
Which strategy should I try?

Solve
Did I follow the plan?
Did I show my work?
Did I write the answer?

Check
Did I use the correct information?
Did I do what was asked?
Is my answer reasonable?

| Facts | Simplify and express in scientific notation. |

$(2 \times 10^6)(3 \times 10^4)$	$(4 \times 10^5)(6 \times 10^4)$	$(2.5 \times 10^3)(3 \times 10^{-6})$
$(4 \times 10^{-3})(2 \times 10^{-4})$	$(5 \times 10^{-5})(3 \times 10^{-4})$	$(2.4 \times 10^{-4})(2 \times 10^6)$

$\dfrac{6 \times 10^8}{3 \times 10^5}$	$\dfrac{5 \times 10^4}{2 \times 10^8}$	$\dfrac{4.2 \times 10^{-3}}{2 \times 10^3}$	$\dfrac{2.4 \times 10^5}{4 \times 10^{-3}}$

| Mental Math |

a.	b.	c.	d.
e.	f.	g.	h.

Problem Solving

Understand

What information am I given?

What am I asked to find or do?

- -

Plan

How can I use the information I am given?

Which strategy should I try?

- -

Solve

Did I follow the plan?

Did I show my work?

Did I write the answer?

- -

Check

Did I use the correct information?

Did I do what was asked?

Is my answer reasonable?

Facts Simplify and express in scientific notation.

$(2 \times 10^6)(3 \times 10^4)$	$(4 \times 10^5)(6 \times 10^4)$	$(2.5 \times 10^3)(3 \times 10^{-6})$
$(4 \times 10^{-3})(2 \times 10^{-4})$	$(5 \times 10^{-5})(3 \times 10^{-4})$	$(2.4 \times 10^{-4})(2 \times 10^6)$

$\dfrac{6 \times 10^8}{3 \times 10^5}$	$\dfrac{5 \times 10^4}{2 \times 10^8}$	$\dfrac{4.2 \times 10^{-3}}{2 \times 10^3}$	$\dfrac{2.4 \times 10^5}{4 \times 10^{-3}}$

Mental Math

a.	**b.**	**c.**	**d.**
e.	**f.**	**g.**	**h.**

Problem Solving

Understand

What information am I given?

What am I asked to find or do?

- -

Plan

How can I use the information I am given?

Which strategy should I try?

- -

Solve

Did I follow the plan?

Did I show my work?

Did I write the answer?

- -

Check

Did I use the correct information?

Did I do what was asked?

Is my answer reasonable?

Facts   Simplify and express in scientific notation.

$(2 \times 10^6)(3 \times 10^4)$	$(4 \times 10^5)(6 \times 10^4)$	$(2.5 \times 10^3)(3 \times 10^{-6})$
$(4 \times 10^{-3})(2 \times 10^{-4})$	$(5 \times 10^{-5})(3 \times 10^{-4})$	$(2.4 \times 10^{-4})(2 \times 10^6)$
$\dfrac{6 \times 10^8}{3 \times 10^5}$	$\dfrac{5 \times 10^4}{2 \times 10^8}$	$\dfrac{4.2 \times 10^{-3}}{2 \times 10^3}$	$\dfrac{2.4 \times 10^5}{4 \times 10^{-3}}$

Mental Math

a.	**b.**	**c.**	**d.**
e.	**f.**	**g.**	**h.**

Problem Solving

Understand

What information am I given?

What am I asked to find or do?

- -

Plan

How can I use the information I am given?

Which strategy should I try?

- -

Solve

Did I follow the plan?

Did I show my work?

Did I write the answer?

- -

Check

Did I use the correct information?

Did I do what was asked?

Is my answer reasonable?

Facts — Simplify.

$2x + x$	$2x - x$	$(2x)(x)$	$\dfrac{2x}{x} =$	$\dfrac{x^2}{x} =$
$8xy + 2xy$	$8xy - 2xy$	$(8xy)(2xy)$	$\dfrac{8xy}{2xy} =$	$\dfrac{8x^2y}{2y} =$
$x + y + x$	$x + y - x$	$(x)(y)(-x)$	$\dfrac{xy}{x} =$	$\dfrac{x^2y^3}{x^2y} =$
$4x + x + 2$	$4x - x - 2$	$(4x)(-x)(-2)$	$\dfrac{-4x}{2x} =$	$\dfrac{4x^3}{2x^2} =$

Mental Math

a.	**b.**	**c.**	**d.**
e.	**f.**	**g.**	**h.**

Problem Solving

Understand

What information am I given?
What am I asked to find or do?

- -

Plan

How can I use the information I am given?
Which strategy should I try?

- -

Solve

Did I follow the plan?
Did I show my work?
Did I write the answer?

- -

Check

Did I use the correct information?
Did I do what was asked?
Is my answer reasonable?

Facts   Simplify.

$2x + x$	$2x - x$	$(2x)(x)$	$\dfrac{2x}{x} =$	$\dfrac{x^2}{x} =$
$8xy + 2xy$	$8xy - 2xy$	$(8xy)(2xy)$	$\dfrac{8xy}{2xy} =$	$\dfrac{8x^2y}{2y} =$
$x + y + x$	$x + y - x$	$(x)(y)(-x)$	$\dfrac{xy}{x} =$	$\dfrac{x^2y^3}{x^2y} =$
$4x + x + 2$	$4x - x - 2$	$(4x)(-x)(-2)$	$\dfrac{-4x}{2x} =$	$\dfrac{4x^3}{2x^2} =$

Mental Math

a.	b.	c.	d.
e.	f.	g.	h.

Problem Solving

Understand
What information am I given?
What am I asked to find or do?

- -

Plan
How can I use the information I am given?
Which strategy should I try?

- -

Solve
Did I follow the plan?
Did I show my work?
Did I write the answer?

- -

Check
Did I use the correct information?
Did I do what was asked?
Is my answer reasonable?

Facts   Simplify.

$2x + x$	$2x - x$	$(2x)(x)$	$\dfrac{2x}{x} =$	$\dfrac{x^2}{x} =$
$8xy + 2xy$	$8xy - 2xy$	$(8xy)(2xy)$	$\dfrac{8xy}{2xy} =$	$\dfrac{8x^2y}{2y} =$
$x + y + x$	$x + y - x$	$(x)(y)(-x)$	$\dfrac{xy}{x} =$	$\dfrac{x^2y^3}{x^2y} =$
$4x + x + 2$	$4x - x - 2$	$(4x)(-x)(-2)$	$\dfrac{-4x}{2x} =$	$\dfrac{4x^3}{2x^2} =$

Mental Math

a.	**b.**	**c.**	**d.**
e.	**f.**	**g.**	**h.**

Problem Solving

Understand

What information am I given?
What am I asked to find or do?

- -

Plan

How can I use the information I am given?
Which strategy should I try?

- -

Solve

Did I follow the plan?
Did I show my work?
Did I write the answer?

- -

Check

Did I use the correct information?
Did I do what was asked?
Is my answer reasonable?

Facts   Simplify.

$2x + x$	$2x - x$	$(2x)(x)$	$\dfrac{2x}{x} =$	$\dfrac{x^2}{x} =$
$8xy + 2xy$	$8xy - 2xy$	$(8xy)(2xy)$	$\dfrac{8xy}{2xy} =$	$\dfrac{8x^2y}{2y} =$
$x + y + x$	$x + y - x$	$(x)(y)(-x)$	$\dfrac{xy}{x} =$	$\dfrac{x^2y^3}{x^2y} =$
$4x + x + 2$	$4x - x - 2$	$(4x)(-x)(-2)$	$\dfrac{-4x}{2x} =$	$\dfrac{4x^3}{2x^2} =$

Mental Math

a.	b.	c.	d.
e.	f.	g.	h.

Problem Solving

Understand

What information am I given?
What am I asked to find or do?

- -

Plan

How can I use the information I am given?
Which strategy should I try?

- -

Solve

Did I follow the plan?
Did I show my work?
Did I write the answer?

- -

Check

Did I use the correct information?
Did I do what was asked?
Is my answer reasonable?

Saxon Math Course 3

Facts   Simplify.

$2x + x$	$2x - x$	$(2x)(x)$	$\dfrac{2x}{x} =$	$\dfrac{x^2}{x} =$
$8xy + 2xy$	$8xy - 2xy$	$(8xy)(2xy)$	$\dfrac{8xy}{2xy} =$	$\dfrac{8x^2y}{2y} =$
$x + y + x$	$x + y - x$	$(x)(y)(-x)$	$\dfrac{xy}{x} =$	$\dfrac{x^2y^3}{x^2y} =$
$4x + x + 2$	$4x - x - 2$	$(4x)(-x)(-2)$	$\dfrac{-4x}{2x} =$	$\dfrac{4x^3}{2x^2} =$

Mental Math

a.	**b.**	**c.**	**d.**
e.	**f.**	**g.**	**h.**

Problem Solving

Understand

What information am I given?

What am I asked to find or do?

- -

Plan

How can I use the information I am given?

Which strategy should I try?

- -

Solve

Did I follow the plan?

Did I show my work?

Did I write the answer?

- -

Check

Did I use the correct information?

Did I do what was asked?

Is my answer reasonable?

Facts

Write each percent as a decimal and as a reduced fraction. Write repeating decimals with a bar over the repetend.

Percent	Decimal	Fraction	Percent	Decimal	Fraction
10%			25%		
90%			20%		
5%			4%		
40%			75%		
$12\frac{1}{2}$%			1%		
50%			$33\frac{1}{3}$%		

Mental Math

a.	b.	c.	d.
e.	f.	g.	h.

Problem Solving

Understand

What information am I given?
What am I asked to find or do?

- -

Plan

How can I use the information I am given?
Which strategy should I try?

- -

Solve

Did I follow the plan?
Did I show my work?
Did I write the answer?

- -

Check

Did I use the correct information?
Did I do what was asked?
Is my answer reasonable?

Facts

Write each percent as a decimal and as a reduced fraction. Write repeating decimals with a bar over the repetend.

Percent	Decimal	Fraction	Percent	Decimal	Fraction
10%			25%		
90%			20%		
5%			4%		
40%			75%		
$12\frac{1}{2}\%$			1%		
50%			$33\frac{1}{3}\%$		

Mental Math

a.	b.	c.	d.
e.	f.	g.	h.

Problem Solving

Understand

What information am I given?

What am I asked to find or do?

- -

Plan

How can I use the information I am given?

Which strategy should I try?

- -

Solve

Did I follow the plan?

Did I show my work?

Did I write the answer?

- -

Check

Did I use the correct information?

Did I do what was asked?

Is my answer reasonable?

| **Facts** | Write each percent as a decimal and as a reduced fraction. Write repeating decimals with a bar over the repetend. |

Percent	Decimal	Fraction	Percent	Decimal	Fraction
10%			25%		
90%			20%		
5%			4%		
40%			75%		
$12\frac{1}{2}$%			1%		
50%			$33\frac{1}{3}$%		

Mental Math			
a.	**b.**	**c.**	**d.**
e.	**f.**	**g.**	**h.**

Problem Solving

Understand
What information am I given?
What am I asked to find or do?

Plan
How can I use the information I am given?
Which strategy should I try?

Solve
Did I follow the plan?
Did I show my work?
Did I write the answer?

Check
Did I use the correct information?
Did I do what was asked?
Is my answer reasonable?

Facts Write each percent as a decimal and as a reduced fraction. Write repeating decimals with a bar over the repetend.

Percent	Decimal	Fraction	Percent	Decimal	Fraction
10%			25%		
90%			20%		
5%			4%		
40%			75%		
$12\frac{1}{2}\%$			1%		
50%			$33\frac{1}{3}\%$		

Mental Math

a.	b.	c.	d.
e.	f.	g.	h.

Problem Solving

Understand
What information am I given?
What am I asked to find or do?

- -

Plan
How can I use the information I am given?
Which strategy should I try?

- -

Solve
Did I follow the plan?
Did I show my work?
Did I write the answer?

- -

Check
Did I use the correct information?
Did I do what was asked?
Is my answer reasonable?

Name _____ Time _____

Facts
Write each percent as a decimal and as a reduced fraction. Write repeating decimals with a bar over the repetend.

Percent	Decimal	Fraction	Percent	Decimal	Fraction
10%			25%		
90%			20%		
5%			4%		
40%			75%		
$12\frac{1}{2}\%$			1%		
50%			$33\frac{1}{3}\%$		

Mental Math

a.	b.	c.	d.
e.	f.	g.	h.

Problem Solving

Understand
What information am I given?
What am I asked to find or do?

- -

Plan
How can I use the information I am given?
Which strategy should I try?

- -

Solve
Did I follow the plan?
Did I show my work?
Did I write the answer?

- -

Check
Did I use the correct information?
Did I do what was asked?
Is my answer reasonable?

Saxon Math Course 3

Facts   U.S. Customary measurement facts: Complete each equivalence.

Linear Measure:

1. 1 foot   = _____ inches

2. 1 yard   = _____ inches

3. 1 yard   = _____ feet

4. 1 mile   = _____ feet

5. 1 mile   = _____ yards

Area:

6. 1 foot^2 = _____ inches^2

7. 1 yard^2 = _____ feet^2

Volume:

8. 1 yard^3 = _____ feet^3

Weight:

9. 1 pound = _____ ounces

10. 1 ton   = _____ pounds

Liquid Measure:

11. 1 pint   = _____ ounces

12. 1 pint   = _____ cups

13. 1 quart = _____ pints

14. 1 gallon = _____ quarts

Temperature:

15. Water freezes at ____ °F.

16. Water boils at ____ °F.

17. Normal body temperature is ____ °F.

Customary to Metric:

18. 1 inch   = _____ centimeters

Mental Math

a.	b.	c.	d.
e.	f.	g.	h.

Problem Solving

Understand

What information am I given?

What am I asked to find or do?

- -

Plan

How can I use the information I am given?

Which strategy should I try?

- -

Solve

Did I follow the plan?

Did I show my work?

Did I write the answer?

- -

Check

Did I use the correct information?

Did I do what was asked?

Is my answer reasonable?

Facts   U.S. Customary measurement facts: Complete each equivalence.

Linear Measure:

1. 1 foot   = _____ inches

2. 1 yard   = _____ inches

3. 1 yard   = _____ feet

4. 1 mile   = _____ feet

5. 1 mile   = _____ yards

Area:

6. 1 foot^2 = _____ inches^2

7. 1 yard^2 = _____ feet^2

Volume:

8. 1 yard^3 = _____ feet^3

Weight:

9. 1 pound = _____ ounces

10. 1 ton   = _____ pounds

Liquid Measure:

11. 1 pint   = _____ ounces

12. 1 pint   = _____ cups

13. 1 quart = _____ pints

14. 1 gallon = _____ quarts

Temperature:

15. Water freezes at ____ °F.

16. Water boils at ____ °F.

17. Normal body temperature is ____ °F.

Customary to Metric:

18. 1 inch   = _____ centimeters

Mental Math

a.	b.	c.	d.
e.	f.	g.	h.

Problem Solving

Understand

What information am I given?
What am I asked to find or do?

- -

Plan

How can I use the information I am given?
Which strategy should I try?

- -

Solve

Did I follow the plan?
Did I show my work?
Did I write the answer?

- -

Check

Did I use the correct information?
Did I do what was asked?
Is my answer reasonable?

Facts   U.S. Customary measurement facts: Complete each equivalence.

Linear Measure:

1. 1 foot   = _____ inches

2. 1 yard   = _____ inches

3. 1 yard   = _____ feet

4. 1 mile   = _____ feet

5. 1 mile   = _____ yards

Area:

6. 1 foot^2 = _____ inches^2

7. 1 yard^2 = _____ feet^2

Volume:

8. 1 yard^3 = _____ feet^3

Weight:

9. 1 pound = _____ ounces

10. 1 ton   = _____ pounds

Liquid Measure:

11. 1 pint   = _____ ounces

12. 1 pint   = _____ cups

13. 1 quart = _____ pints

14. 1 gallon = _____ quarts

Temperature:

15. Water freezes at ____ °F.

16. Water boils at ____ °F.

17. Normal body temperature is ____ °F.

Customary to Metric:

18. 1 inch   = _____ centimeters

Mental Math

a.	b.	c.	d.
e.	f.	g.	h.

Problem Solving

Understand

What information am I given?
What am I asked to find or do?

Plan

How can I use the information I am given?
Which strategy should I try?

Solve

Did I follow the plan?
Did I show my work?
Did I write the answer?

Check

Did I use the correct information?
Did I do what was asked?
Is my answer reasonable?

Facts	U.S. Customary measurement facts: Complete each equivalence.

Linear Measure:

1. 1 foot = _____ inches

2. 1 yard = _____ inches

3. 1 yard = _____ feet

4. 1 mile = _____ feet

5. 1 mile = _____ yards

Area:

6. 1 foot^2 = _____ inches^2

7. 1 yard^2 = _____ feet^2

Volume:

8. 1 yard^3 = _____ feet^3

Weight:

9. 1 pound = _____ ounces

10. 1 ton = _____ pounds

Liquid Measure:

11. 1 pint = _____ ounces

12. 1 pint = _____ cups

13. 1 quart = _____ pints

14. 1 gallon = _____ quarts

Temperature:

15. Water freezes at ____ °F.

16. Water boils at ____ °F.

17. Normal body temperature is ____ °F.

Customary to Metric:

18. 1 inch = _____ centimeters

Mental Math			
a.	**b.**	**c.**	**d.**
e.	**f.**	**g.**	**h.**

Problem Solving

Understand

What information am I given?

What am I asked to find or do?

- -

Plan

How can I use the information I am given?

Which strategy should I try?

- -

Solve

Did I follow the plan?

Did I show my work?

Did I write the answer?

- -

Check

Did I use the correct information?

Did I do what was asked?

Is my answer reasonable?

Facts   U.S. Customary measurement facts: Complete each equivalence.

Linear Measure:

1. 1 foot   =_____ inches

2. 1 yard   =_____ inches

3. 1 yard   =_____ feet

4. 1 mile   =_____ feet

5. 1 mile   =_____ yards

Area:

6. 1 foot^2 =_____ inches^2

7. 1 yard^2 =_____ feet^2

Volume:

8. 1 yard^3 =_____ feet^3

Weight:

9. 1 pound =_____ ounces

10. 1 ton   =_____ pounds

Liquid Measure:

11. 1 pint   =_____ ounces

12. 1 pint   =_____ cups

13. 1 quart =_____ pints

14. 1 gallon =_____ quarts

Temperature:

15. Water freezes at ____ °F.

16. Water boils at ____ °F.

17. Normal body temperature is ____ °F.

Customary to Metric:

18. 1 inch   =_____ centimeters

Mental Math

a.	b.	c.	d.
e.	f.	g.	h.

Problem Solving

Understand
What information am I given?
What am I asked to find or do?

- -

Plan
How can I use the information I am given?
Which strategy should I try?

- -

Solve
Did I follow the plan?
Did I show my work?
Did I write the answer?

- -

Check
Did I use the correct information?
Did I do what was asked?
Is my answer reasonable?

Facts	Write each fraction as a decimal and as a percent. Write repeating decimals with a bar over the repetend.

Fraction	Decimal	Percent	Fraction	Decimal	Percent
$\frac{1}{2}$			$\frac{1}{6}$		
$\frac{1}{3}$			$\frac{1}{8}$		
$\frac{2}{3}$			$\frac{1}{9}$		
$\frac{1}{4}$			$\frac{1}{10}$		
$\frac{3}{4}$			$\frac{1}{50}$		
$\frac{1}{5}$			$\frac{1}{100}$		

Mental Math			
a.	b.	c.	d.
e.	f.	g.	h.

Problem Solving

Understand

What information am I given?

What am I asked to find or do?

Plan

How can I use the information I am given?

Which strategy should I try?

Solve

Did I follow the plan?

Did I show my work?

Did I write the answer?

Check

Did I use the correct information?

Did I do what was asked?

Is my answer reasonable?

Facts

Write each fraction as a decimal and as a percent.
Write repeating decimals with a bar over the repetend.

Fraction	Decimal	Percent	Fraction	Decimal	Percent
$\frac{1}{2}$			$\frac{1}{6}$		
$\frac{1}{3}$			$\frac{1}{8}$		
$\frac{2}{3}$			$\frac{1}{9}$		
$\frac{1}{4}$			$\frac{1}{10}$		
$\frac{3}{4}$			$\frac{1}{50}$		
$\frac{1}{5}$			$\frac{1}{100}$		

Mental Math

a.	b.	c.	d.
e.	f.	g.	h.

Problem Solving

Understand
What information am I given?
What am I asked to find or do?

Plan
How can I use the information I am given?
Which strategy should I try?

Solve
Did I follow the plan?
Did I show my work?
Did I write the answer?

Check
Did I use the correct information?
Did I do what was asked?
Is my answer reasonable?

Facts

Write each fraction as a decimal and as a percent.
Write repeating decimals with a bar over the repetend.

Fraction	Decimal	Percent	Fraction	Decimal	Percent
$\frac{1}{2}$			$\frac{1}{6}$		
$\frac{1}{3}$			$\frac{1}{8}$		
$\frac{2}{3}$			$\frac{1}{9}$		
$\frac{1}{4}$			$\frac{1}{10}$		
$\frac{3}{4}$			$\frac{1}{50}$		
$\frac{1}{5}$			$\frac{1}{100}$		

Mental Math

a.	b.	c.	d.
e.	f.	g.	h.

Problem Solving

Understand

What information am I given?
What am I asked to find or do?

Plan

How can I use the information I am given?
Which strategy should I try?

Solve

Did I follow the plan?
Did I show my work?
Did I write the answer?

Check

Did I use the correct information?
Did I do what was asked?
Is my answer reasonable?

Facts Write each fraction as a decimal and as a percent.
Write repeating decimals with a bar over the repetend.

Fraction	Decimal	Percent	Fraction	Decimal	Percent
$\frac{1}{2}$			$\frac{1}{6}$		
$\frac{1}{3}$			$\frac{1}{8}$		
$\frac{2}{3}$			$\frac{1}{9}$		
$\frac{1}{4}$			$\frac{1}{10}$		
$\frac{3}{4}$			$\frac{1}{50}$		
$\frac{1}{5}$			$\frac{1}{100}$		

Mental Math

a.	b.	c.	d.
e.	f.	g.	h.

Problem Solving

Understand

What information am I given?

What am I asked to find or do?

Plan

How can I use the information I am given?

Which strategy should I try?

Solve

Did I follow the plan?

Did I show my work?

Did I write the answer?

Check

Did I use the correct information?

Did I do what was asked?

Is my answer reasonable?

© Houghton Mifflin Harcourt Publishing Company and Stephen Hake

Facts

Write each fraction as a decimal and as a percent.
Write repeating decimals with a bar over the repetend.

Fraction	Decimal	Percent	Fraction	Decimal	Percent
$\frac{1}{2}$			$\frac{1}{6}$		
$\frac{1}{3}$			$\frac{1}{8}$		
$\frac{2}{3}$			$\frac{1}{9}$		
$\frac{1}{4}$			$\frac{1}{10}$		
$\frac{3}{4}$			$\frac{1}{50}$		
$\frac{1}{5}$			$\frac{1}{100}$		

Mental Math

a.	b.	c.	d.
e.	f.	g.	h.

Problem Solving

Understand

What information am I given?
What am I asked to find or do?

Plan

How can I use the information I am given?
Which strategy should I try?

Solve

Did I follow the plan?
Did I show my work?
Did I write the answer?

Check

Did I use the correct information?
Did I do what was asked?
Is my answer reasonable?

Facts	Write the formula for the geometric concept.	
circumference of a circle	area of a circle	perimeter of a rectangle
area of a parallelogram	area of a triangle	Pythagorean Theorem
area of a trapezoid	volume of a prism or cylinder	volume of a pyramid or cone

Mental Math

a.	b.	c.	d.
e.	f.	g.	h.

Problem Solving

Understand
What information am I given?
What am I asked to find or do?

- -

Plan
How can I use the information I am given?
Which strategy should I try?

- -

Solve
Did I follow the plan?
Did I show my work?
Did I write the answer?

- -

Check
Did I use the correct information?
Did I do what was asked?
Is my answer reasonable?

Facts	Write the formula for the geometric concept.	
circumference of a circle	area of a circle	perimeter of a rectangle
area of a parallelogram	area of a triangle	Pythagorean Theorem
area of a trapezoid	volume of a prism or cylinder	volume of a pyramid or cone

Mental Math

a.	b.	c.	d.
e.	f.	g.	h.

Problem Solving

Understand

What information am I given?

What am I asked to find or do?

- -

Plan

How can I use the information I am given?

Which strategy should I try?

- -

Solve

Did I follow the plan?

Did I show my work?

Did I write the answer?

- -

Check

Did I use the correct information?

Did I do what was asked?

Is my answer reasonable?

Facts Write the formula for the geometric concept.

circumference of a circle	area of a circle	perimeter of a rectangle
area of a parallelogram	area of a triangle	Pythagorean Theorem
area of a trapezoid	volume of a prism or cylinder	volume of a pyramid or cone

Mental Math

a.	**b.**	**c.**	**d.**
e.	**f.**	**g.**	**h.**

Problem Solving

Understand

What information am I given?

What am I asked to find or do?

- -

Plan

How can I use the information I am given?

Which strategy should I try?

- -

Solve

Did I follow the plan?

Did I show my work?

Did I write the answer?

- -

Check

Did I use the correct information?

Did I do what was asked?

Is my answer reasonable?

| Facts | Write the formula for the geometric concept. |

circumference of a circle	area of a circle	perimeter of a rectangle
area of a parallelogram	area of a triangle	Pythagorean Theorem
area of a trapezoid	volume of a prism or cylinder	volume of a pyramid or cone

Mental Math

a.	b.	c.	d.
e.	f.	g.	h.

Problem Solving

Understand

What information am I given?
What am I asked to find or do?

Plan

How can I use the information I am given?
Which strategy should I try?

Solve

Did I follow the plan?
Did I show my work?
Did I write the answer?

Check

Did I use the correct information?
Did I do what was asked?
Is my answer reasonable?

Facts Write the formula for the geometric concept.

circumference of a circle	area of a circle	perimeter of a rectangle
area of a parallelogram	area of a triangle	Pythagorean Theorem
area of a trapezoid	volume of a prism or cylinder	volume of a pyramid or cone

Mental Math

a.	b.	c.	d.
e.	f.	g.	h.

Problem Solving

Understand
What information am I given?
What am I asked to find or do?

- -

Plan
How can I use the information I am given?
Which strategy should I try?

- -

Solve
Did I follow the plan?
Did I show my work?
Did I write the answer?

- -

Check
Did I use the correct information?
Did I do what was asked?
Is my answer reasonable?

Facts   Metric Measurement Facts: Complete each equivalence.

Linear Measure:

1. 1 centimeter = _____ millimeters

2. 1 meter   = _____ centimeters

3. 1 meter   = _____ millimeters

4. 1 kilometer = _____ meters

Area and Volume:

5. 1 meter^2 = _____ centimeters^2

6. 1 kilometer^2 = _____ meters^2

7. 1 meter^3 = _____ centimeters^3

Mass:

8. 1 gram   = _____ milligrams

9. 1 kilogram   = _____ grams

10. 1 metric ton = _____ kilograms

Capacity:

11. 1 liter = _____ milliliters (mL).

12. One milliliter of water has a volume of _____

13. and a mass of _____ .

14. One thousand cm^3 of water fills a _____ -liter container and has a

15. mass of _____ kilogram.

Temperature:

16. Water freezes at ___ °C.

17. Water boils at ___ °C.

18. Normal body temperature is ___ °C.

Mental Math

a.	b.	c.	d.
e.	f.	g.	h.

Problem Solving

Understand

What information am I given?
What am I asked to find or do?

- -

Plan

How can I use the information I am given?
Which strategy should I try?

- -

Solve

Did I follow the plan?
Did I show my work?
Did I write the answer?

- -

Check

Did I use the correct information?
Did I do what was asked?
Is my answer reasonable?

Facts   Metric Measurement Facts: Complete each equivalence.

Linear Measure:

1. 1 centimeter = _____ millimeters

2. 1 meter = _____ centimeters

3. 1 meter = _____ millimeters

4. 1 kilometer = _____ meters

Area and Volume:

5. 1 meter^2 = _____ centimeters^2

6. 1 kilometer^2 = _____ meters^2

7. 1 meter^3 = _____ centimeters^3

Mass:

8. 1 gram = _____ milligrams

9. 1 kilogram = _____ grams

10. 1 metric ton = _____ kilograms

Capacity:

11. 1 liter = _____ milliliters (mL).

12. One milliliter of water has a volume of _____

13. and a mass of _____.

14. One thousand cm^3 of water fills a _____ -liter container and has a

15. mass of _____ kilogram.

Temperature:

16. Water freezes at ___ °C.

17. Water boils at ___ °C.

18. Normal body temperature is ___ °C.

Mental Math

a.	b.	c.	d.
e.	f.	g.	h.

Problem Solving

Understand
What information am I given?
What am I asked to find or do?

Plan
How can I use the information I am given?
Which strategy should I try?

Solve
Did I follow the plan?
Did I show my work?
Did I write the answer?

Check
Did I use the correct information?
Did I do what was asked?
Is my answer reasonable?

Facts Metric Measurement Facts: Complete each equivalence.

Linear Measure:

1. 1 centimeter = _____ millimeters

2. 1 meter = _____ centimeters

3. 1 meter = _____ millimeters

4. 1 kilometer = _____ meters

Area and Volume:

5. 1 meter^2 = _____ centimeters^2

6. 1 kilometer^2 = _____ meters^2

7. 1 meter^3 = _____ centimeters^3

Mass:

8. 1 gram = _____ milligrams

9. 1 kilogram = _____ grams

10. 1 metric ton = _____ kilograms

Capacity:

11. 1 liter = _____ milliliters (mL).

12. One milliliter of water has a volume of _____

13. and a mass of _____ .

14. One thousand cm^3 of water fills a _____ -liter container and has a

15. mass of _____ kilogram.

Temperature:

16. Water freezes at ___ °C.

17. Water boils at ___ °C.

18. Normal body temperature is ___ °C.

Mental Math

a.	b.	c.	d.
e.	f.	g.	h.

Problem Solving

Understand

What information am I given?
What am I asked to find or do?

- -

Plan

How can I use the information I am given?
Which strategy should I try?

- -

Solve

Did I follow the plan?
Did I show my work?
Did I write the answer?

- -

Check

Did I use the correct information?
Did I do what was asked?
Is my answer reasonable?

Facts   Metric Measurement Facts: Complete each equivalence.

Linear Measure:

1. 1 centimeter = _____ millimeters

2. 1 meter = _____ centimeters

3. 1 meter = _____ millimeters

4. 1 kilometer = _____ meters

Area and Volume:

5. 1 meter^2 = _____ centimeters^2

6. 1 kilometer^2 = _____ meters^2

7. 1 meter^3 = _____ centimeters^3

Mass:

8. 1 gram = _____ milligrams

9. 1 kilogram = _____ grams

10. 1 metric ton = _____ kilograms

Capacity:

11. 1 liter = _____ milliliters (mL).

12. One milliliter of water has a volume of _____

13. and a mass of _____ .

14. One thousand cm^3 of water fills a _____ -liter container and has a

15. mass of _____ kilogram.

Temperature:

16. Water freezes at ___ °C.

17. Water boils at ___ °C.

18. Normal body temperature is ___ °C.

Mental Math

a.	b.	c.	d.
e.	f.	g.	h.

Problem Solving

Understand

What information am I given?
What am I asked to find or do?

- -

Plan

How can I use the information I am given?
Which strategy should I try?

- -

Solve

Did I follow the plan?
Did I show my work?
Did I write the answer?

- -

Check

Did I use the correct information?
Did I do what was asked?
Is my answer reasonable?

Facts	Metric Measurement Facts: Complete each equivalence.

Linear Measure:

1. 1 centimeter = _____ millimeters

2. 1 meter   = _____ centimeters

3. 1 meter   = _____ millimeters

4. 1 kilometer = _____ meters

Area and Volume:

5. 1 meter^2 = _____ centimeters^2

6. 1 kilometer^2 = _____ meters^2

7. 1 meter^3 = _____ centimeters^3

Mass:

8. 1 gram   = _____ milligrams

9. 1 kilogram = _____ grams

10. 1 metric ton = _____ kilograms

Capacity:

11. 1 liter = _____ milliliters (mL).

12. One milliliter of water has a volume of _____

13. and a mass of _____.

14. One thousand cm^3 of water fills a _____ -liter container and has a

15. mass of _____ kilogram.

Temperature:

16. Water freezes at ____ °C.

17. Water boils at ____ °C.

18. Normal body temperature is ___ °C.

Mental Math

a.	b.	c.	d.
e.	f.	g.	h.

Problem Solving

Understand

What information am I given?
What am I asked to find or do?

- -

Plan

How can I use the information I am given?
Which strategy should I try?

- -

Solve

Did I follow the plan?
Did I show my work?
Did I write the answer?

- -

Check

Did I use the correct information?
Did I do what was asked?
Is my answer reasonable?

Facts Simplify.

$\sqrt{8}$	$\sqrt{18}$	$\sqrt{50}$	$\sqrt{12}$
$\sqrt{200}$	$\sqrt{32}$	$\sqrt{45}$	$\sqrt{75}$
$\sqrt{48}$	$\sqrt{20}$	$\sqrt{90}$	$\sqrt{72}$

Mental Math

a.	b.	c.	d.
e.	f.	g.	h.

Problem Solving

Understand

What information am I given?

What am I asked to find or do?

Plan

How can I use the information I am given?

Which strategy should I try?

Solve

Did I follow the plan?

Did I show my work?

Did I write the answer?

Check

Did I use the correct information?

Did I do what was asked?

Is my answer reasonable?

Facts	Simplify.		
$\sqrt{8}$	$\sqrt{18}$	$\sqrt{50}$	$\sqrt{12}$
$\sqrt{200}$	$\sqrt{32}$	$\sqrt{45}$	$\sqrt{75}$
$\sqrt{48}$	$\sqrt{20}$	$\sqrt{90}$	$\sqrt{72}$

Mental Math

a.	b.	c.	d.
e.	f.	g.	h.

Problem Solving

Understand

What information am I given?

What am I asked to find or do?

Plan

How can I use the information I am given?

Which strategy should I try?

Solve

Did I follow the plan?

Did I show my work?

Did I write the answer?

Check

Did I use the correct information?

Did I do what was asked?

Is my answer reasonable?

Facts Simplify.

$\sqrt{8}$	$\sqrt{18}$	$\sqrt{50}$	$\sqrt{12}$
$\sqrt{200}$	$\sqrt{32}$	$\sqrt{45}$	$\sqrt{75}$
$\sqrt{48}$	$\sqrt{20}$	$\sqrt{90}$	$\sqrt{72}$

Mental Math

a.	b.	c.	d.
e.	f.	g.	h.

Problem Solving

Understand
What information am I given?
What am I asked to find or do?

- -

Plan
How can I use the information I am given?
Which strategy should I try?

- -

Solve
Did I follow the plan?
Did I show my work?
Did I write the answer?

- -

Check
Did I use the correct information?
Did I do what was asked?
Is my answer reasonable?

Facts   Simplify.

$\sqrt{8}$	$\sqrt{18}$	$\sqrt{50}$	$\sqrt{12}$
$\sqrt{200}$	$\sqrt{32}$	$\sqrt{45}$	$\sqrt{75}$
$\sqrt{48}$	$\sqrt{20}$	$\sqrt{90}$	$\sqrt{72}$

Mental Math

a.	b.	c.	d.
e.	f.	g.	h.

Problem Solving

Understand
What information am I given?
What am I asked to find or do?

Plan
How can I use the information I am given?
Which strategy should I try?

Solve
Did I follow the plan?
Did I show my work?
Did I write the answer?

Check
Did I use the correct information?
Did I do what was asked?
Is my answer reasonable?

Facts	Simplify.		

$\sqrt{8}$	$\sqrt{18}$	$\sqrt{50}$	$\sqrt{12}$
$\sqrt{200}$	$\sqrt{32}$	$\sqrt{45}$	$\sqrt{75}$
$\sqrt{48}$	$\sqrt{20}$	$\sqrt{90}$	$\sqrt{72}$

Mental Math

a.	b.	c.	d.
e.	f.	g.	h.

Problem Solving

Understand

What information am I given?

What am I asked to find or do?

Plan

How can I use the information I am given?

Which strategy should I try?

Solve

Did I follow the plan?

Did I show my work?

Did I write the answer?

Check

Did I use the correct information?

Did I do what was asked?

Is my answer reasonable?

Facts   Find each product.

$(x + 3)(x + 3)$	$(x - 3)(x - 3)$	$(x + 3)(x - 3)$
$(x + 2)(x + 3)$	$(x + 2)(x - 3)$	$(x - 2)(x - 3)$
$(x + 4)(x + 5)$	$(x - 4)(x + 5)$	$(x - 4)(x - 5)$

Mental Math

a.	b.	c.	d.
e.	f.	g.	h.

Problem Solving

Understand

What information am I given?

What am I asked to find or do?

Plan

How can I use the information I am given?

Which strategy should I try?

Solve

Did I follow the plan?

Did I show my work?

Did I write the answer?

Check

Did I use the correct information?

Did I do what was asked?

Is my answer reasonable?

Facts   Find each product.

$(x + 3)(x + 3)$	$(x - 3)(x - 3)$	$(x + 3)(x - 3)$
$(x + 2)(x + 3)$	$(x + 2)(x - 3)$	$(x - 2)(x - 3)$
$(x + 4)(x + 5)$	$(x - 4)(x + 5)$	$(x - 4)(x - 5)$

Mental Math

a.	**b.**	**c.**	**d.**
e.	**f.**	**g.**	**h.**

Problem Solving

Understand
What information am I given?
What am I asked to find or do?

- -

Plan
How can I use the information I am given?
Which strategy should I try?

- -

Solve
Did I follow the plan?
Did I show my work?
Did I write the answer?

- -

Check
Did I use the correct information?
Did I do what was asked?
Is my answer reasonable?

Facts   Find each product.

$(x + 3)(x + 3)$	$(x - 3)(x - 3)$	$(x + 3)(x - 3)$
$(x + 2)(x + 3)$	$(x + 2)(x - 3)$	$(x - 2)(x - 3)$
$(x + 4)(x + 5)$	$(x - 4)(x + 5)$	$(x - 4)(x - 5)$

Mental Math

a.	b.	c.	d.
e.	f.	g.	h.

Problem Solving

Understand

What information am I given?
What am I asked to find or do?

Plan

How can I use the information I am given?
Which strategy should I try?

Solve

Did I follow the plan?
Did I show my work?
Did I write the answer?

Check

Did I use the correct information?
Did I do what was asked?
Is my answer reasonable?

Facts   Find each product.

$(x + 3)(x + 3)$	$(x - 3)(x - 3)$	$(x + 3)(x - 3)$
$(x + 2)(x + 3)$	$(x + 2)(x - 3)$	$(x - 2)(x - 3)$
$(x + 4)(x + 5)$	$(x - 4)(x + 5)$	$(x - 4)(x - 5)$

Mental Math

a.	b.	c.	d.
e.	f.	g.	h.

Problem Solving

Understand

What information am I given?

What am I asked to find or do?

Plan

How can I use the information I am given?

Which strategy should I try?

Solve

Did I follow the plan?

Did I show my work?

Did I write the answer?

Check

Did I use the correct information?

Did I do what was asked?

Is my answer reasonable?

Name _____ Time _____

Facts   Find each product.

$(x + 3)(x + 3)$	$(x - 3)(x - 3)$	$(x + 3)(x - 3)$
$(x + 2)(x + 3)$	$(x + 2)(x - 3)$	$(x - 2)(x - 3)$
$(x + 4)(x + 5)$	$(x - 4)(x + 5)$	$(x - 4)(x - 5)$

Mental Math

a.	b.	c.	d.
e.	f.	g.	h.

Problem Solving

Understand

What information am I given?
What am I asked to find or do?

Plan

How can I use the information I am given?
Which strategy should I try?

Solve

Did I follow the plan?
Did I show my work?
Did I write the answer?

Check

Did I use the correct information?
Did I do what was asked?
Is my answer reasonable?

Saxon Math Course 3